Children Finding Faith

FRANCIS BRIDGER

Scripture Union
130 City Road, London EC1V 2NJ

To Renee, Rebecca, Samantha, Simon
and Kevin who have all inspired me in
the writing of this book.

© Francis Bridger 1988

First published 1988

ISBN 0 86201 460 3

British Library Cataloguing in Publication Data

Bridger, Francis
  Children finding faith.
  1. Children. Christian life
  I. Title
  248.8′2

  ISBN 0–86201–460–3

Phototypeset by Input Typesetting Ltd, London
Printed and bound in Great Britain by
Cox and Wyman Ltd., Reading.

Contents

Preface

This book is written primarily for three kinds of reader: those who are full-time children's workers; those who, like me, have been involved with children's missions and holiday clubs in school holidays; and those who are concerned with ministry to children in its broadest sense, whether in family worship, Sunday school, junior church or elsewhere. Others may find it helpful and if so, I shall be delighted. But it is with these three groups in mind that I have written.

The task of ministering to children is both a great privilege and a great responsibility. The opportunity to share Christ with children in their formative years can be decisive. We therefore need to be, in Jesus' words, 'as wise as serpents and as harmless as doves' (Matt 10:16). Working with children requires special skills and sensitivity. The influence an adult can have is potentially enormous.

It is for this reason that I have attempted to bring together two vital aspects of effective children's ministry. In part one we look at a number of approaches to understanding *how children develop*. Much work has been done in recent years in this area but little is readily accessible to the non-expert. By means of a fictional narrative about two children, I have sought to bring together a number of important insights which can inform our understanding and make us better children's workers.

But this gives rise to unavoidable theological questions. Many of these have been part of ongoing debate among evangelists and children's workers for some time. However, the discussion of child development throws them into particularly sharp relief and also introduces new questions. Part two is therefore given over to looking at these in some detail, all the time seeking to make connections with the practical dimension.

It is my hope, therefore, that the reader will find himself or herself discovering new things, thinking new thoughts, and developing new insights into children's ministry. If this book enables the reader to achieve any of these it will have succeeded in its purpose.

Francis Bridger
St John's College, Nottingham

Acknowledgements

No book is complete without acknowledgement of those who have made it possible. Although many people have been involved in one way or another, I particularly wish to thank the following: the Revd Doug Chaplin for some theological stimulus when I found it hard to start; Mrs Pat Travis for crucial advice at a key stage and for reading and commenting on the draft; the Revd Sylvia Griffiths for advising on issues faced by children's workers; the Revd John Gooding for pressing me on questions about the church as family; the Revd Dr David Atkinson and Mrs Suzanne Atkinson for reading the draft and making many helpful suggestions; Mrs Rebecca Totterdell for inviting me to write in the first place and for continuing editorial support; and, most of all, my wife Renee for her theological and practical comments and for sacrificing me to the word processor. To others who have had a hand in this project, but whom I have not named, I also render my thanks.

I also wish to thank Edward Arnold Ltd for permission to quote from Carol Mumford's *Young Children and Religion*.

PART ONE

Children finding faith

Modern views of the way faith develops
throughout a child's life.

1
Babyhood

Day one to twelve months

The beginning of faith in the earliest months of life:
The experiences of Lee and Lizzie

The nature of faith:
  1. *Faith as believing*
  2. *Faith as trusting*
  3. *Faith as doing*

Lee

The first year of life is a whirlpool of experiences for baby Lee. He does not know it yet, but the basic patterns of his future are being formed in these early months. Most basic of all is the experience of simple trust, and it is from this that Lee will develop the capacity for faith. As with many things, this experience began at birth.

Like the rest of the human race, Lee will never consciously remember his birth but, tucked away in the depths of his subconscious, is the memory of that first experience of separation. For the first time, he was no longer physically tied to his mother, no longer surrounded by the warmth, comfort and protection of her womb, but now, instead, a separate being. At the moment of his birth Lee became distinct but dependent. In years to come, he will be told that when he curls up in a warm bed with his knees beneath his chin, he is unconsciously returning to the security of his womb. But for now, Lee knows nothing of that. At only a few weeks old, he instinctively turns to his mother for everything he needs, both physical and emotional. He may be separate from her but he is not separated.

Fortunately, Lee's mother loves him dearly. He is not her first child and neither will he be the last. But he is to be her only son. She does not yet know this (which is just as well) and her love for him, although different from that which she lavished upon his older sisters, is no more and no less free and generous. So with no more than instinct to guide him, Lee has, in his first year, come to know the meaning of love and trust in the little world which fills the boundaries of his existence.

This trust has been directed towards *persons*. Or to be exact, one person – Lee's mother. Whenever he has needed her, she has been there. Food, warmth, safety have all been found in her arms. As time has gone by, Lee has discovered that these things come regularly and reliably. At first, he was fearful if he woke and his mother was not there. When first this happened, he experienced sheer terror. But he soon learned that his source of love was never far away. The constant experiences of touching and being touched, cuddling and being cuddled, holding onto and being held have assured Lee that the world is orderly, kind and trustworthy. They have given Lee a far deeper understanding of love and trust than any later form of words will be able to.

Lee therefore knows what it means to have faith. To be sure, he doesn't have any idea what the words mean – words mean nothing to him yet – but he knows what it is to trust and to have that trust honoured. Lee has taken his first step of faith.

But there are other things Lee has been learning. For the first few months, the world to him was one sensation after another. He loved the colours, the shapes, the noise, the attention – he was captivated by them all. Everything was the world and the world was everything. And he was in the middle of it.

But slowly Lee came to distinguish one object from another. What he was later to call a pig was distinct from what he would discover to be a duck or a teddy.

And another thing. By the time he was nine months old, Lee had begun to realize that these objects could be hidden, and he wanted to search for them. Only a few months earlier, it had been a question of 'out of sight, out of mind'. If they were hidden, he just forgot about them. He had no image of them in his mind. But now, wonder of wonders, teddy and ball and all the rest of them stuck in his head. If mother removed them, Lee was soon to be found crawling around in search of them. The world had become a place of permanent objects, persons and places.

Throughout this period, Lee began to discover the use of his body. Within the continuous flow of sensations and objects he slowly started to distinguish different things and experiences. Lee also began to discover that he could react to and even influence them. He found out, for instance, that if he reached out for teddy and flexed his fingers, he could hold teddy's hand and pull him over. Bit by bit this action came to be repeated until Lee understood simple acts of co-ordination.

Not all was easy, though, and some actions brought pain. When he persistently pushed his dinner off the highchair, Lee soon learned that some patterns of behaviour were definitely not to be repeated!

. . . and Lizzie

Now let us turn to Elizabeth. Although born in the same ward as Lee, she is not destined to be so fortunate in her early months or years. For Lizzie (as she will come to be known) is not really wanted. She was an 'accident'. Her mother is married but wishes she wasn't. The youngest of a family of six, Lizzie's mum has had a lifetime of being last. But despite this, she soldiered on to gain some secretarial qualifications and left school to take up a decent job with a firm of metal box manufacturers.

No sooner had she done so than she fell in love with a boy at work and quickly got married. The thought of starting a family could not have been further from her mind. But nature was to overrule and along came Lizzie within a year.

At eighteen, Lizzie's mother is furious and frustrated. Her career has ended before it has had a chance to begin and she sees herself as tied down for life. Although the baby is not to blame, Lizzie remains the ever-present symbol of the trap in which her mother is caught.

It is little surprise, then, that Lizzie receives none of the warmth and love lavished upon Lee. Not for her the constant affection shown by word and touch. Not even the regularity of feeding can overcome the intense rejection which her mother radiates towards her. From the beginning, baby Elizabeth experiences the most bitter feeling of all – that of not being wanted. As the years ripen, she will come to know the pain which only those who have been rejected from birth can know. In time, she will come to say for herself the words which have not been *spoken* by her mother but which do not need voicing for they silently fill the air: 'I wish Lizzie had never been born'.

In the meantime Lizzie, like Lee, learns the basic control of her limbs and the permanency of objects. But she does not know the permanency of parenthood. For her mother has found a way out of her dilemma: Lizzie is farmed out to a childminder while her mother resumes her career. Her father doesn't object: his wife was becoming impossible to live with and the second income helps pay the mortgage.

Of course, it need not have been like this. Plenty of mothers go out to work and still spend valuable time with their children.

But this can succeed only when there is a genuine sharing of love, affection and trust. Likewise, a child may find warmth and care with a minder. But the point about Lizzie, as with so many children, is that in neither case was this true. As a result her sense of rejection was to remain with her for years to come.

Within eighteen months of their being born, then, we have two infants whose lives could not be more at variance: Lee who is loved and valued and Lizzie who is unloved and rejected. The one learns faith through the most fundamental of human experiences: the love and affection of the doting parent who sees her child as a gift and a treasure. The other knows nothing of faith for she does not know how (or whom) to trust in a world where adults seem only to care for themselves. When, in time, Lee and Lizzie come to hear of their heavenly parent whom they will be told loves them like a father, their differing infant experiences of parenthood will, like a hidden, underground river, flow through their personalities to influence for good or ill their respective capacities for faith.

What is faith?

The stories of Lee and Lizzie are not uncommon. Although fictional, they are drawn from real life – from the observations and recollections of many hundreds of people, compiled in the course of research into child development. We do not have to be researchers, however, to recognize the Lees and Lizzies of our lives. For most of us, Lee and Lizzie will ring true. For some who read this book, they will ring true all too painfully.

The central point in this early infant period is that children unconsciously absorb their attitudes of trust through their relationship with their parents, particularly the mother. The foundations of faith are being laid even at this early stage. A child who does not learn how to trust adults now will have difficulty trusting anybody at more than a superficial level later on.

This extends to trust in God. A valuable exercise in any congregation would be to find out how many adults who once made professions of faith in Christ and then dropped away had experienced disrupted patterns of trust in their early months or years.

We should not be surprised if high proportions of children, and adults with emotional problems that go back to their childhood, find it difficult to stick with their initial commitment to Christ. Their desire to follow him may be completely genuine and they may long to love and be loved both by God and by Christian people. But, in the crucial first months of their lives, they have missed out on the fundamental experiences of trust-building. As a result they find it hard to trust and to believe that others trust them at the deep levels of their beings. Most of all, they cannot feel that God loves or trusts them. For if even those who brought them into the world do not accept them, why should God?

In this situation the minister, evangelist or friend has to realize that the vital stage of trust-building which was lost in infancy must now be made up for in the life of the child or adult convert. The rejection or lack of acceptance experienced during infancy has to be replaced by the *experiencing* of constant, patient love. This will not be a matter simply of words. The statement, 'We trust you, please trust us', however kindly meant, will not be enough, for the damage that has to be mended has taken place at a much deeper level. The hurt of that child or adult can only begin to be unlearned when they experience our continuous *acceptance* of whatever they can offer – no matter how irregular or incomplete this may be. In many ways, it is not the adult or older child who is acting and speaking to us at this point: it is the infant inside, who has never experienced acceptance and trust. The word of the Lord to us will therefore be, 'Be patient, be gentle even as I am patient and gentle.' It will not be, 'Castigate and threaten this sinner for backsliding.'

It is imperative, therefore, that we grasp the crucial importance of the first months of life and the spiritual effects of the relationships established during them. The capacity for faith is a wonderful but fragile thing.

Faith, however, is not dependent simply on human development. We are also forced back to *theological* questions: What is faith? How does the development of the capacity for trust relate to biblical teaching about what it means to have faith in God? We shall spend the rest of this chapter examining a theological understanding of faith in the light of what we have begun to see from the study of child development.

The story of Lee and Lizzie so far is the story of the *human* dimension of faith. But this does not invalidate or squeeze out the divine. Because God is creator as well as redeemer, the natural processes of human development are part of his ordering of the world. The human and divine aspects of faith are bound together like Siamese twins. So before we go on to look at how faith can develop throughout a person's life, we must establish a definition of faith which is true both to Christian theology and to how we develop as persons.

The Bible makes it clear that faith is a gift of God. It cannot be won or earned – it is given by God (Phil 1:29; 1 Cor 2:5). But how does this fit in with the idea of faith development, especially in the lives of children who may not be consciously aware of having received faith?

The answer lies in understanding faith as part of God's gift in creation as well as his gift in salvation. The two are intimately connected because God is the Lord of both, as the incarnation demonstrates. When, therefore, we think of children as somehow possessing faith 'naturally', we do not mean that they do so independently of God. He is the author of their lives from the beginning and it is by his grace in creation that they (and we) are capable of trust and of response both to other human beings and to God himself.

So faith is, from start to finish, a gift just as the whole of life is a gift. It does not begin at the moment we accept Christ as Saviour, though in the work of salvation God takes the faith he has given us as part of his creation and by grace transforms it into saving faith in his Son. Saving faith arises out of the way God has made us in creation: it is all of a piece, the nature of which is gift.

The capacity for faith which is given to us as God's creatures, however, is a humanly exercised faith. Although it is given by God, it is nevertheless we who exercise it. James Fowler has proposed that we should understand this human exercise of faith as an activity which enables us to make sense of our lives. Faith, he says, is 'our way of finding coherence in and giving meaning to the multiple forces and relations that make up our lives.' Faith is thus 'a person's way of seeing him or herself in relation to others against a background of shared purpose and meaning.'[1]

Fowler's definition has the advantage of treating faith seriously as a human activity, and provided it is understood in a theological context such as we have discussed, it is useful. However, we must insist that it is not the *activity* of faith alone that is decisive: equally important before God is its *content* or *object*. A Hindu, Buddhist, Moslem or humanist may all exercise faith in their different ways. But it is only through faith in the risen Christ that salvation may be found. The capacity for faith given at birth must lead to faith in Jesus for its fulfilment.

Thomas H Groome has argued that Christian faith must be seen in three Christ-centred dimensions: faith as believing, faith as trusting and faith as doing.[2] When all are present in the life of the Christian, he is exercising truly biblical faith.

1. Faith as believing

It is a Sunday morning. The congregation is half-way through the weekly service of Holy Communion. The preacher has just finished his sermon and the vicar stands up to lead his flock in making their response to the word of God. At this point, the Anglican Alternative Service Book is quite explicit about what form such a response should take: it should take the form of saying the Creed.

In this way, week by week, the equation of faith with the holding of theological propositions is reinforced. Even the most unintellectual believer cannot escape the conclusion that faith is first and foremost an act of the mind. 'I believe in (God . . . Jesus . . . the Holy Spirit. . .) . . .' is almost invariably translated to mean 'I believe the following about (God . . . Jesus . . . the Holy Spirit. . .) . . .' This emphasis upon faith as an intellectual activity has frequently been overplayed. But the importance of believing in doctrinal truths should not be understated. Throughout history Christianity has claimed that being a Christian cannot be just a matter of feelings. There must be a core of beliefs which can be propositionally stated and which must be assented to if the believer is to be regarded as an authentic follower of Christ.

The reason for this is straightforward. The church in the first four centuries quickly and repeatedly found that all kinds of groups were ready to claim the authority of Christ for an assortment of views (many of them heretical), especially when it came to controversy about the person of Jesus. Time after time it became essential for the church to set out what it believed in order to sort out the doctrinal sheep from the goats. A glance at the history of heresies shows how necessary this process was. The same is true today with the growth and spread of cults such as Jehovah's Witnesses, Mormons, Moonies and the like. Without a clear idea of the truths concerning God, Christ and the Spirit, Christians would be fair game for any sect which came along. As Groome has commented: 'The *activity* of Christian faith, therefore, requires in part a firm *conviction* about the truths proposed as essential beliefs of the Christian faith.'[3]

Historically, however, this emphasis on the role of the *mind* in the activity of faith came to present a major difficulty. By the time of the Reformation, the intellectual component of faith was regarded as the most important. The Reformers stressed afresh the importance of the heart and will in addition to the intellect, but in the late seventeenth century a new movement in secular philosophy began which came to elevate reason as supreme. This movement was known as the Enlightenment.

The Enlightenment swept over Christian Europe like a tidal wave. It proclaimed human reason as the supreme instrument of progress and the means by which individuals could be freed from superstition. (Christianity was held up as an example of such superstition.) Those who elevated reason above all else were consequently known as Rationalists – a term and a philosophy which has continued down to the present day.

The Christian church reacted to the Enlightenment in two ways. On one hand there were those who spurned reason in favour of reliance upon an inward work of the Spirit, a kind of 'inner light' as the Quakers called it. This had the enormous advantage of bypassing reason altogether and thereby avoiding any need to confront the Rationalists on their own ground. When challenged about the intellectual validity or coherence of their faith, all the proponents of the inner light (or *illuminists* as they were known) had to do was to take refuge in an inward revelation from God or a direct experience of the Spirit. They did not need to justify themselves in the court of reason: they merely had to say, 'The Lord has told me this and you cannot disprove it.'

The second Christian reaction to Rationalism was to assimilate it. This was achieved usually by claiming that reason had been given by God as his divinely appointed instrument for understanding the world and his will. By itself, this claim was not incompatible with Christian faith. It is perfectly possible, and indeed important, to see reason as *one* of the means God has given us to understand his orderly and coherent creation and to discover his will. But the belief arose, and is still held today, that God could *only* be understood and related to by means of human Reason (with a capital R). Revelation quickly became squeezed out along with miracles. Neither of these could be accepted unless they could be squashed into a Rationalist mould. So the feeding of the five thousand was reinterpreted as an act of communal sharing, misunderstood by the Gospel writers; and miracles such as the calming of the storm were seen as the normal workings of nature dressed up to prove the divinity of the man Jesus.

It is little surprise that the English church of the eighteenth century came close to death and that only the combination of the Wesleyan, Evangelical and Anglo-Catholic revivals of the eighteenth and nineteenth centuries saved it from becoming merely Rationalism with a religious face.

What we face today, therefore, are the effects of this struggle. If we picture faith as a tripod, believing the truth of theological propositions is one rightful leg, but it is only one. Trusting and doing form the others; and all three are necessary. Unfortunately, owing to the impact of, and hangover from, the Enlightenment, Christians all too often find themselves forced into a polarized choice between faith as intellectual assent and faith as inner emotional commitment. In biblical terms it does not need to be like this: faith can be both belief about, and commitment to, the One who is both the Truth and the Lord of heart and mind.

2. Faith as trusting

Consider the following statements:

(a) 'Good morning Mr Jones. I trust that you are well today.'
(b) 'Trust and obey, for there's no other way to be happy in Jesus, but to trust and obey.'

Both contain the word 'trust' but there is a difference: (a) represents faith in a state of affairs. We trust *that* poor old Mr Jones is not under the weather. In (b), however, we are exhorted to trust *in* a person – Jesus. Being happy is tied to a personal relationship of faith and obedience.

Of course, the two may be brought together when we trust that a state of affairs is satisfactory because we have faith in the person responsible for them:

> 'I trust you will find this cake to your taste, Vicar. My wife baked it this morning and you can always trust her to turn out a winner.'

When we speak of faith in God as 'trusting', we have in mind this combined meaning. We not only trust what God says or does, more fundamentally we trust *him* as a person. As we reflect on this, we begin to move away from a purely intellectual and propositional definition of faith. Christian believing becomes more than assent to a series of statements about God: it moves into the area of personal relationship.

James Fowler has helpfully characterized this as *covenantal faith*.[4] A covenant is an agreement or bond between two persons. Both parties are pledged to each other and there is a flow of trust in both directions. Each has faith in the other that what he promises will be fulfilled. Covenantal faith is thus rooted in relationships which are trustworthy and dependable.

The example *par excellence* favoured by the biblical writers was the covenant between God and Abraham. (Note that the partners in a covenantal relationship do not have to be equals. It is enough that they engage in a bond based on mutual trust.) Between Genesis chapters 12 and 17 (supplemented by Paul in Romans 4), we read that God took the initiative in establishing a covenant with Abraham and that Abraham responded in faith.

This covenant involved two-way trust. On Abraham's side, he had to believe God's promise that despite his age and the barrenness of his wife Sarah, Abraham would become the father of many nations. Moreover, he had to trust when God commanded him to leave his home and travel to Canaan where he had no kin, no wealth and no security. The trust God demanded could not have been greater: 'Leave your country, your people and your father's household. . .' (Gen 12:1). How many of us today would listen to a sudden command from an unknown God to do away with all our familiar security and travel abroad where we are promised blessings impossible by any natural standard?

Yet, as Paul says, 'Against all hope, Abraham in hope believed and so became the father of many nations, just as it had been said to him' (Rom 4:18). Covenantal faith won for him blessing and righteousness. God, for his part, trusted Abraham. Abraham's shady dealings with his wife in Egypt make it clear that he was as humanly frail and fearful as the rest of us. Yet the fact is that Abraham persevered and in faith reached the promised land. The trust God placed in him was fulfilled.

But the story of Abraham illustrates a crucial aspect of covenantal faith in God. Paul reminds us that despite the natural odds against the fulfilment of God's promise to him, Abraham 'did not waver through unbelief regarding the promise of God, but *was strengthened in his faith* and gave glory to God' (Rom 4:20; italics mine). In his weakness, Abraham found that far from being abandoned by God, God built up his faith and thereby cemented the covenantal relationship. Abraham was not left on his own to fail. The exercise of trust within the divine covenant is thus wholly a matter of grace. We are back to the notion of faith as a gift.

The covenant between God and man serves as a model for all forms of covenantal faith. It contains the characteristics essential to a bond between persons: it is personal, mutual and gracious. A healthy parent-offspring relationship will exhibit all these in the first months of life. As we have seen, it is here that the human source of faith is to be found.

3. Faith as doing

Luther described the letter of James as 'an epistle of straw'. He believed its emphasis upon good works undermined the Reformation recovery of Pauline teaching on grace and faith. For Luther, surrounded by the corrupt philosophy of salvation by works which had come to characterize the medieval church, the rediscovery of grace and faith brought liberation and hope.

But however right Luther may have been in his context, we cannot ignore the fact that for the New Testament writers, faith and works were inseparable. The mere profession of faith in God must be backed up by evidence of a new way of life – the life of the kingdom. 'Not everyone who says to me "Lord, Lord," will enter the kingdom of heaven, but only he who does the will of my Father who is in heaven' (Matt 7:21). Likewise, Paul's great teaching on salvation by faith in the first eleven chapters of Romans is followed immediately by four chapters of practical instruction as to what it means to live out salvation in behaviour and relationships.

Faith, then, is not a matter of *feeling* right before God. It is grateful acceptance of the gift of redemption, and a readiness to do all that follows from it. It is a matter of saying, 'I am saved by the mercy of God. Now what must I do to live out the new life that is within me?' James 2:14–17 has the answer:

'What good is it, my brothers, if a man claims to have faith but has no deeds? Can such faith save him? Suppose a brother or sister is without clothes and daily food. If one of you says, "Go, I wish you well; keep warm and well fed," but does nothing about his physical needs, what good is it? In the same way, faith by itself, if it is not accompanied by action, is dead.'

It is an unfortunate side effect of the reaction against Rationalism and the retreat into a feelings-based faith, that much modern Christianity has failed to take this biblical command seriously. Such has been the fear either of lapsing into salvation by works or of falling into a dependence upon human reason, that we have neglected the 'doing' aspect of faith.

Of course, it is fatally easy to substitute a works-centred religiosity for a living faith in the free grace of God. But the antidote for this is not to avoid the 'doing' aspect of faith but to understand that our relationship with God through Christ requires us to be doers of the word and not hearers only (James 1:22). If we are to be truly biblical in our discipleship we have no choice.

Faith, then, contains these three dimensions: believing, trusting and doing. If the task of the evangelist is to present the gospel so that people may *come* to faith, then we must recognize that evangelistic strategy has to be geared up to enabling individuals to *grow* in it. Evangelism which concentrates on only one dimension to the exclusion or minimizing of the other two is untrue to its name and untrue to God.

CONCLUSION

It is clear that of these three dimensions of faith the second – trusting – is the key to relating faith to infants. The categories of believing and doing cannot possibly apply since they require abilities which young children do not yet have.

This helps us to understand the importance of the early months, up to one and a half or two years. As we have observed, it is in this period that the 'trusting' leg of the faith tripod is formed. When we later come to speak of God as our heavenly Father and we encourage children (or adults for that matter) to trust him, it will be to the deep wells of infant trust that we shall be calling. For children like Lee, our appeal is likely to find an echoing response. They will at least know what it means to have experienced trust, acceptance and love at the hands of a parent. For children like Lizzie, however, the likelihood is much less. That is not to say that the Lizzies of this world are incapable of responding to the gospel: by the grace of God they are. But the kind of response they make and the emotional soil out of which it arises may be very thin indeed. We should not be surprised to find a response based on a desire to please or to be accepted by adults. The nature of trust in these circumstances will be fragile and precarious and we shall need to be as wise as serpents and as harmless as doves in seeking to strengthen it.

Is there, then, any evangelism which is appropriate to young infants? The answer, perhaps surprisingly, is 'yes'. But it will consist entirely of a relationship of love. It will contain no intellectual message nor will it call for a response other than to trust in the human who shows love. It will be a gospel of cuddles and softly spoken words. These are the seeds out of which, by the grace of God, fuller faith may develop.

NOTES TO CHAPTER 1

1. James Fowler, *Stages of Faith*, New York: Harper & Row 1981, p. 4.
2. Thomas H Groome, *Christian Religious Education*, New York: Harper & Row 1980, p 57.
3. Groome, as above.
4. For a development of this idea, see Fowler, above, pp 16–23.

2
Infancy

Thirteen months to six years

The development of faith during infancy and the relationship between experience and belief:

Growing up
   Lee's confidence
   Lizzie's unhappiness
Patterns of faith development
   Capacity for trust
   Relating outside the family
The gospel and children's capacities
   Story
   Understanding in terms of experience
   Unconnected logic

Growing up

Lee's confidence

Babyhood gave way to infancy. With this came a torrent of new experiences – like the time when Lee spoke his first word. He was about fifteen months old. Predictably enough the word had been 'Dada'. But what struck Lee's parents was the way he then called every other man 'Dada'. Lee could simply not distinguish: he just thought that all men were called 'Dada'.

Communication

It was not always to be the case. As Lee grew more fluent in using words (he did not always understand their meanings) he discovered a much greater power over his world. He could command and control the objects around him. He could tell his parents what he wanted. He could be precise about where it hurt when he felt ill. And, above all, he could communicate with his friends. Language was the gateway to society and his place in it.

Independence

Then there was the other great occasion of independence – Lee's first unaided walk. It was not very far but enough to set him on the road to mobility and autonomy. By four or five he had completely mastered the control of his limbs. Lee had begun to establish himself as an independent person in his own right.

Playschool came – and went. Lee enjoyed every moment of it and there he took another step forward in understanding. For the first time, he came to realize that the world consisted of more than his own family. It slowly dawned on him that he could no longer get away with many of the things he had done at home. The playschool leaders were not so easily manipulated as his mother and his sisters. Lee learned, the hard way, that a tantrum would not be rewarded with a biscuit and a glass of milk but with some stern (although loving) words while other children got on happily with their finger painting. He was going to have to take account of others.

Of course, Lee *tried* to get his own way. The world might now be larger than that of his infancy and he might no longer be the centre of it all the time, but he could still act as if he were.

Identity and will

This theory was put to the test in the summer of the year Lee went to school. By this time, Lee had established for himself a sense of identity and will. It even extended to Ted, his favourite bear. The two of them would sit down together each afternoon to discuss the day at playschool and other important matters such as what they might have for tea. But it was not until the day before the trip to the seaside that Lee's parents realized quite how strong their son's identity had become.

It had all begun with a conversation about what they should take on a day trip to the seaside. Lee insisted that he should take his tricycle. Dad pointed out that there wouldn't be room in the car; Lee was sure there would be. And so it went on. After a short time, tempers were rising on both sides. Lee was determined the trike should go and Dad was determined it shouldn't. Needless to say, as with many such exchanges, Dad imposed his authority and it all ended in tears and an early bedtime. The tricycle did not go the next day but Lee's parents were careful to note their son's independence of spirit and wisely took it into account in future.

Lee's next great experience was school. He quickly settled and gained a reputation as 'a strong-minded and determined little boy', a comment occasioned by Lee's insistence after two days that he could make his own way to the toilet, thank you very much. (Fortunately it was next to his classroom.)

Imagination

It was in the year before starting school, and during his first year there, that Lee developed a love for stories. Although he used to enjoy watching television, his love for hearing stories was just as great. Through story books at home and at school, he entered enchanted worlds of magic, excitement and adventure. He heard about pigs and wicked wolves, little old ladies who lived in vinegar bottles, witches and wizards, fairy princes and princesses. His imagination took off.

No less important at this time, however, was Lee's growing sense of awe, wonder and beauty. As his powers of imagination grew, so did his capacity for these. Without realizing it, he was beginning to develop the capacity to reach towards God.

Lee also heard about Jesus.

To Lee all these stories were rolled into one. At first he got them mixed up so much that he couldn't quite remember whether the pigs lived in a vinegar bottle or which house the witch had magicked into rubble. And where was it that Jesus and God lived? Oh yes, it was in the forest near the little people, wasn't it?

Slowly, Lee began to get the stories sorted out in his mind. But even by the time he went to junior school, he still wasn't sure what kind of magic Jesus had used to feed all those people and heal the sick men and women. And what was all this about Jesus and God living up in the sky? Daddy had flown up in the sky when he went to visit Aunty Jane in America. Had he seen Jesus on the way? He must have done, Lee supposed, but Daddy hadn't said so.

Little by little, the building blocks of Lee's personality were being put into place. It would be some years before the construction would be anything like complete, but the shape of the building was becoming clear. It might be redesigned or built upon further, but it would never be dismantled.

Lizzie's unhappiness

Humiliation

If Lee had a happy infancy, however, Lizzie suffered the opposite. Her mother came to like or love her no more as time passed. It didn't help that the childminding service was arranged on a rota so that from one day to the next Lizzie never had the same adult to relate to. To make it harder, she was sometimes left with a reluctant aunt who didn't want Lizzie any more than her mother. It was here that Lizzie experienced her first humiliation.

The occasion was little more than a minor inconvenience, Lizzie soiled herself by accident (she was three). Her aunt was extremely angry, smacked her and sent her to bed for the rest of the afternoon. From that moment on, Lizzie became fastidious in toilet matters. She also lived in fear and trembling of her aunt and would even pretend illness rather than be left there for the day.

By the age of four, then, Lizzie had not found a single adult to whom she could entrust herself freely and totally. It seemed that the adult world, far from offering security, reassurance and confidence, presented only rejection, humiliation and anxiety.

Play

Things changed with the advent of playgroup. Lizzie's mother was a bit late in getting her into this but the nine months she spent there were the best of her life. For the first time she mixed with other children of her own age. There were interesting things to do and there were *toys*.

Now Lizzie had never been allowed many toys. In fact, her mother frowned upon play as something wasteful and useless. Lizzie's main stimulus had been the television. But at playgroup a whole new world opened up to her. She would spend hours just going from toy to toy, playing for a time with each one in turn. Dolls, bears, donkeys, ponies, telephones, tricycles, houses – they were all sheer joy. The end of each day was a heartbreak. Would she be allowed to see them all again?

Alternative lives

It was during this time that Lizzie met the first adult who seemed interested in her. This was the mother of another girl at play-group, Wendy. Unlike Lizzie, Wendy was not an only child; she had a brother two years older and a sister one year younger. She and Lizzie became friends.

One day Wendy invited Lizzie home for tea. Lizzie's mum was only too glad, so the two little girls, escorted by Wendy's mother, excitedly set out for Wendy's home.

Her time there was better than she had ever known before. There were delicious things for tea and Wendy's mum and dad showed a kindness she had never met. Lizzie had no way of knowing whether this was always the case but she was happy enough to accept the kindness of the moment. But what struck her most of all was an incident involving Wendy's brother Colin. It was quite unlike anything Lizzie had experienced before.

Colin was a very active boy. He was always running about, shouting and making himself known to whoever would listen.

People usually did listen for he had a way of winning you over even against your better judgment. But Colin did not like playing with girls, least of all his younger sister. So when Wendy came home with another girl, he decided to make his attitude clear. The result was a spider down Wendy's neck (he did nothing to Lizzie) which produced howls of terror and rage.

This, startling though it was, was not the thing which most left its mark on Lizzie: it was the way Colin's mum dealt with him. To be sure, Colin got a smack and a telling off but there was no sense of rejection in the punishment. Once the matter was dealt with, it was regarded as finished. The errant boy was accepted once more. Wendy kept her distance from him for a time, but that was a precaution as much as a sulk. As Lizzie came to know Wendy's family better, she came to see that punishment could be combined with fairness and love; that it did not have to be a matter of capricious and unpredictable rage and that she and her friends might not be such hopelessly bad people after all.

Had she known it, Lizzie was beginning to acquire positive images of herself, of parenthood and family life, and was beginning to learn the meaning of trust.

Confusion

By the end of her first year at school, Lizzie was living in four worlds: home which she dreaded and disliked; school, which she liked but in which she was not confident; Wendy's, which she loved and wished she could live in all the time; and the inner world of fantasy and imagination, which she fell into when she wanted to escape from the realities of home. Like Lee, Lizzie revelled in stories. But unlike Lee, they became the springboard for daydreams to distract her from whatever might be going on at that time. More and more, she found her teacher recalling her from some magic world where all grown-ups were kind (except for the wicked witch) and children could play for ever. By her seventh birthday (by which time she, too, had moved up to junior school), Lizzie was truly mixed up.

Patterns of faith development

What patterns of faith development can we discern within the life stories of Lee and Lizzie so far? How should these affect our attitude to children's ministry?

Capacity for trust

Emotionally, we continue to see the importance of the parent in the formation of a child's capacity for trust. The love and attention which had surrounded Lee from his birth continued through his infancy. Adults were neither a threat nor a source of fear for him, as they were for Lizzie. They offered acceptance, confidence and affection.

This proved crucial in Lee's development as an independent personality. By late infancy he had become aware that the world was not simply a matter of himself and his desires: it comprised other 'selves' who also had *their* lives and desires. The love of his family enabled him to begin to establish *his* identity in its own right without fear that he would be humiliated or squashed.

For Lizzie, life told a different story. Her early rejection at the hands of all the adults who mattered, and who were responsible for her, instilled in her a deep mistrust of the adult world. The adults who dominated her infant world either failed or refused to accept her, while the constantly changing rota of uninterested carers was bound to produce an acute sense of worthlessness. Had Lizzie heard about the love of God, or about the notion of God as her heavenly Father, it is unlikely that emotionally she would have been able to respond in any but a negative way.

The most significant factor in creating trust-faith, therefore, is the primary experience of the child-parent relationship. It is difficult to overstate the importance of this, especially in the early months of life.

Relating outside the family

It is in the infant stage, however, that children begin to learn to relate to others outside the family. This introduces an entirely new set of considerations. No longer is reality confined to the narrow range of people who have surrounded the child from birth. He must now come to terms with wider society. For both

Lee and Lizzie, the playgroup provided the bridge into a social environment not centred on the family. But whereas Lee was ready to co-operate (albeit to a limited extent) with other children, Lizzie needed to make up for the many practical deprivations of her early years. Having been deprived of toys and play facilities, she desperately needed to feel free among such things in her new setting of playschool. Consequently, her capacity and readiness for making relationships was limited. Even more than most children of that age, she was still turned in upon herself. (This is a characteristic of all infants up to about seven but is accentuated in those like Lizzie.)

We noticed, too, the formation of identity in this stage. Lee's tussle with his parents about the trip to the seaside represented not so much a streak of stubborn naughtiness (however much it seemed that way to the adults) as an assertion of independent personhood. This is crucial if the development of a mature capacity for choice and judgment is ever to take place. Children who become content to rely on the judgment of others or upon the consensus of their peers have failed to develop a fully independent identity. This frequently has its roots in infancy. In adult years, even among Christians, this can lead to shallow faith which, under pressure, is unable to stand.

Significant, too, is the combination of firmness with fairness. Wendy's mother knew this in her punishment of Colin. But the reason it impressed Lizzie was that she had known only treatment which was arbitrary and rejecting. The idea of punishment operating within a framework of justice and love was unknown to her. Again, this will have implications for her understanding of, and reaction to, Christian teaching about God, Jesus and salvation.

These factors go to make up the setting into which knowledge of Jesus will arrive. They constitute the soil in which the seeds of the gospel will be planted. But what kind of seeds are appropriate for children moving through this stage?

The gospel and children's capacities

Story
The most important fact is that whatever the *content* of Christian

teaching may be, its most fruitful *form* will be that of the story. We have seen how both Lee and Lizzie lap up the medium of story. It is *the* way in which children of this age learn. We must recognize, too, that the child at this stage of development finds it almost impossible to disentangle one kind of story from another. Jesus, God and fairies are all of a piece. They all inhabit the same world. There is no difference between miracles and magic.

One implication for the evangelist or children's worker is that at this stage of development the use of miracle stories can be extremely misleading. Because they are not yet capable of distinguishing between magic and the miraculous, children will inevitably confuse the two and Jesus will be seen as another kind of wizard or magician. No amount of telling the child that Jesus is not really magical will make any difference. The child's framework of understanding and interpretation will still put miracles in the category of magic. He is capable of no other way of thinking. Even if we successfully get a child to say it is not so, he will not believe it in any meaningful sense: he will simply be repeating what an adult has told him to say. We might as well get him to recite the theory of relativity.

There is, however, one important proviso to this. As children grow older, they can gradually distinguish between what the significant adults in their lives believe to be true and what they see as 'make-believe'. A child whose parents do believe in miracles, and who are able to make a distinction for the child between magic and the power of God, is much more likely to develop a healthier view of miracles than a child whose parents disbelieve or have not got beyond the magical stage themselves. This underlines what we have noted earlier, namely that the *context* of teaching is the key to a child's understanding.

Understanding in terms of experience

A second aspect of a child's capacity in this period is the way in which everything is interpreted in terms of his or her day to day experiences. Carol Mumford records the response of one six year old to the wonder of the sun. Note how the child understands the new experience only in terms of what he has already experienced:

I think it is marvellous that the sun stays up in the sky.
I think some string is holding it up. Why doesn't it fall down?[1]

Or the five year old who watched her mother get dinner ready
one day and asked what God has for his dinner. The conversation
which followed went like this:

Mum: God doesn't have any dinner.
Mary: Well if he doesn't have any dinner, does he have an egg
for his tea?
Mum: (wondering how to explain)
God doesn't have any tea either, dear. He doesn't need
to eat because he hasn't got a body.
Mary: (having pondered on this)
I see what you mean. His legs come right up to his
neck.[2]

The implication is not simply that we should avoid using figurative language about God but that invariably the child will form
an image of God based on his own experience of the world around
him. Information drawn from scripture or from the adult's
experience will be translated by the child into terms which make
sense within the child's life world or within the mental world he
has constructed from stories, television and other sources. Even
where the *words* (such as God) are identical with adult vocabulary,
the images and meanings attached to them will be different.

Unconnected logic

Thirdly (this is related to the previous point), we need to realize
that just as children at this stage of the developmental sequence
possess a particular emotional and psychological structure, so
they also possess a corresponding *logical* structure. The most
characteristic features of the way children reason in this stage are
fluidity and apparent unconnectedness. Different bits of a child's
thinking pop up in a seemingly unrelated fashion. It is all a
jumble. To the adult mind, his statements often contain no logical
coherence and there is no connection between them. God gets
mixed in with all sorts of natural and historical events in random
fashion. James Fowler gives a good example of this. In his book
Stages of Faith he records a conversation held with six year old

Freddy about what a family might see deep in the woods. It illustrates well the points we have been making:[3]

Freddy: They see ′ – you can see deers, you can get sunshine. You see beautiful trees. You see lakes and you see clear streams.

Interviewer: Well tell me, how did all of these trees and animals and lakes get there?

Freddy: By rain. . . Mothers get the babies. The sun shines through the clouds and that's a lot of fun. Yeah, the stream and the water lakes. The lakes – the lakes get um, more – the forest – you have a deep hole and then it rains and then when it's full enough they – it's a – it's a lake. But when it gets stinky you can't swim.

Interviewer: Oh I see. Well why do you think we have trees and animals?

Freddy: 'cause God made them.

Interviewer: I see. Why do you think he made them?

Freddy: 'cause. 'cause there's two reasons why. Number one is 'cause trees give off oxygen and number two is 'cause animals protect other animals.

Interviewer: I see, I see. Well why are there people?

Freddy: Uh – I don't know.

Interviewer: Can you think what it would be like if there weren't any people?

Freddy: The beautiful world would become ugly.

Interviewer: How come?

Freddy: 'cause nobody would be down and the world would be ugly.

Interviewer: Yeah?

Freddy: I think it would be like in the old days and things.

Interviewer: And what was it like in the old days?

Freddy: Like there was big holdups. There was wagons going fast.

Interviewer: But what – what about even before that? What if there weren't any people anywhere?

Freddy: Just animals? I think it would be like – be like an animal world.

Interviewer: Would that be good?

Freddy: No, if there weren't any people, who would be the animals?

Interviewer: Well, how did people get here?

Freddy: They – they got here from God? That's all I know about the old days.

This interview reveals clearly how 'unadult' a child's logical system actually is. Freddy jumps from one point to another, answering the questions by drawing on what he has seen on television or heard in stories. His description of the old days is a blatant example of this: holdups and wagons. Likewise, his conception of animals seems that they are rather like humans inside animal skins: 'if there weren't any people, who would be the animals?' he asks. Perhaps we see here shades of the Disney culture.

The child in late infancy therefore has images of God which are extremely confused. Given that the child constructs his understanding of God from everyday experience, we should not be surprised if such images are crudely human:[4]

Interviewer: Can you tell me what God looks like?
Freddy: He has a light shirt on he has brown hair, he has brown eyelashes.
Interviewer: (looking at two statues of Christ)
Does everybody think God looks like that?
Freddy: Mmm . . . not when he gets a haircut.

CONCLUSION

Round about seven, the average child reaches a boundary. He begins to move from infancy to juniorhood. This is marked publicly by the transition from infant to junior school. A new phase is assumed to have begun. There is no turning back.

But life-long patterns of personality have been established. As we have seen, the first stages of child and child-faith development are characterized by the impact of personal relationships. It is these, particularly between a child and its parents, which are crucial in the formation of identity, outlook on the world, and the capacity for covenantal faith.

However we look at it, there are considerable implications for evangelism and ministry to children. We need to be aware that almost everything we say will be reinterpreted according to what the child already knows by experience or has had passed down to him (which is a form of experience). What effect will this have upon the content of our message? We shall close this chapter with some suggestions for teaching children at this stage of development.

Negatively, we shall:

1. Be careful about teaching miracle stories. Nothing sounds more magical than the story of Daniel in the lions' den or the feeding of the 5000. We are not in the business of associating God with magic.

2. Not teach material which requires adult modes of thinking or logic. This rules out abstract concepts such as sin, salvation, or redemption. It is highly unlikely that these can be recast in infant terms, even if plenty of illustrations are used.

3. Be careful in our use of parables. These are complex pieces of theological teaching. The fact that they are in story form should not blind us to the fact that they require symbolic logic far in excess of infant capacity.

4. Shun religious fables in which animals are invested with human or divine characteristics. This can be confusing and lead to theological hang-ups at a later stage. If God is associated with the magical or mythical, he may be rejected when the child comes to reject myth as mere make-believe.

5. Resist pressure to call for adult-style commitment. It is a

wholly inappropriate response to expect from this age group and may do considerable damage.

Positively, we shall:

1. Show acceptance of a child, however difficult he or she may be. This does not mean we shall avoid reproving him but we shall try to act like Wendy's mum – in love as well as justice.

2. Build on images and relationships of trust which have made up a child's experience. If he associates the Christian worker with a warm and trusting relationship, he will be more ready to trust God.

3. Not worry if the content of our message says little about Christ the Saviour. It is faith defined as trust rather than knowledge which carries meaning for the child at this stage of development.

4. Focus on teaching which is easily understood in terms of a child's everyday world. This will probably centre on relationships and simple experiences of nature. (God loves us like Mummy. God makes the trees grow.)

5. Construct teaching programmes which centre on stories of persons and personal relationships. Stories about Jesus will be chosen to illustrate his love for people and children.

6. Teach in stories. This will require skilful storytelling which captures children's imaginations. Looking at story books written for 4–6 year olds will be helpful here.

7. Look for responses appropriate to the age and stage of development of each child.

To sum up, then. While it would be a mistake to think of the early years of childhood in conventional evangelistic terms, it would be equally wrong to assume that there is no form of evangelism appropriate to this period. As the chart below shows, there is a direct connection between a child's formative xperiences of relational love and its subsequent capacity for spiritual understanding and growth. The evangelist or children's worker should not be a Billy Graham but that does not mean he has no role.

The relationship between experience and belief

A relationship of shared trust, love and care

IS THE FOUNDATION FOR   *IS THE FOUNDATION FOR*

Security, responsiveness to others, dependability, openness, trust shown towards other people.	**PAVES THE WAY FOR FAITH IN**	Seeing God as personal, trustworthy, consistent, dependable, gracious.
Being valued as a person.	⟶	Seeing God's love for individuals.
Acceptance of self and others.	⟶	Being aware of God's forgiveness, cleansing and renewal. New life in Christ.
Putting things right when a relationship is broken or wrongdoing committed.	⟶	Repentance and reconciliation.
Acceptance of punishment which is fair and does not lead to rejection.	⟶	Understanding the vicarious death of Christ.
Desire to preserve and enjoy relationships.	⟶	Dialogue with God. Obedience to God's will.
Mutual giving in relationships.	⟶	Service to God in response to his grace.

NOTES TO CHAPTER 2

1. Carol Mumford, *Young Children and Religion*, London: Edward Arnold 1982, p 35.
2. Mumford, as above, p 60.
3. James Fowler, *Stages of Faith*, New York: Harper & Row 1981, p 124.
4. Fowler, as above, p 127.

3
The junior years

Age seven to ten years

The characteristics of junior age children; a pivotal age for faith development:

Characteristics of the junior
  Increasing understanding
  Empathy and justice
  New loyalties
The effect on faith development
  1. Believing
  2. Trusting
  3. Doing
The shift in focus
Taking spiritual stock
  Experienced faith

Characteristics of the junior

The junior school child is a wonder to behold. For Lee and Lizzie, juniorhood was a period of amazing growth in every conceivable way. Little more than enlarged infants when they entered the school, they emerged some four years later well on the way to adolescence.

Increasing understanding

In common with their friends, they simply gobbled up information during this time. Lee once spent all day ploughing through *The Guinness Book of Records* 'just because I'm interested' (as he had remarked to his surprised mother). He also joined the local library and could be seen regularly each Saturday morning borrowing three or four books which he duly read in the course of the next week. He was not particularly studious – he simply liked finding out things.

Lizzie was equally curious (particularly about little-known facts) but she did not read much. Her favourite medium was television. Although she watched all sorts of programmes ('It keeps her quiet', was her mother's reaction), it was not just a question of cartoons and the *Dukes of Hazzard*. She also watched *Blue Peter* and even *John Craven's Newsround* because they contained lots of interesting information and human interest stories. She would never have read *The Guinness Book of Records* but she did watch *Recordbreakers*. To her surprise, she found that she and Lee knew the same facts.

This drive for knowledge was accompanied by other effects. Shortly before the Christmas following her seventh birthday, Lizzie had been challenged by Colin, Wendy's older brother, about Santa Claus. 'Surely you don't *still* believe in Father Christmas,' he had crowed, 'I gave up that kids' stuff last year.' At the time, Lizzie had been shocked: she had always believed in Santa Claus because that's what adults had always said. Now here was Colin saying the opposite! Whom should she believe?

Lizzie asked Wendy's mum who encouraged her not to worry too much about Colin: 'He loves to tease, you know,' was her reply. And that was that. Or was it? Needless to say, Father Christmas went the same way for Lizzie as he had for Colin and, by the time she was eight, Lizzie had come to learn that the fairy tale world of her early childhood was not the reality she had once believed. She still enjoyed the richness of fantasy stories, but that is what they now were – make-believe which excited and thrilled the imagination but which firmly belonged inside the head: they were not part of the 'real' world.

Knowledge, then, for Lizzie and Lee took the form of 'real' knowledge about the 'real' world you could see, touch and handle. If it wasn't 'real', it wasn't true.

This was reinforced by the way their reasoning powers were developing. By the third year at junior school, both children had become interested in science. It was here that you could perform simple experiments and that was fun. But it was much more than that. Experiments enabled Lee, Lizzie and their contemporaries to understand the idea of cause and effect.

From then on, the notion of cause and effect became firmly embedded in their understanding. This was especially true for Lizzie. She could see that it was a fundamental principle of how the world functioned. Until then she had just accepted that things happened: now she began to look for the causes. Her logic had taken a leap forward. In her teenage years, this belief in the necessity of cause and effect was to make her highly sceptical of anything whose cause could not be demonstrated. But for the time being she simply absorbed it into her expanding world of knowledge and experience.

Lee and Lizzie had moved on from seeing the world in terms of disconnected events to thinking in sequence. If you ever asked them to explain what they had done that day, the answer always went something like: 'We did this, then we did that, then we both went off and did something else, then we came back again and then we watched TV, then we had something to eat, then we went out to play and after that we called on her cousin. . .'

We all know this kind of conversation. It can take hours. But the fact is that for children such as Lizzie and Lee, the junior age is one in which the world ceases to be a jumble of unrelated events remembered at random and becomes instead a narrative world in which experiences are made sense of by recounting them in copious detail in the order in which they happened. Anyone who has listened to a summary of a film by a child of this age will know that it requires a great deal of patience on the part of the listener. It can also help if you have already seen the film!

So whenever Lee's mum asked him what kind of day he had had at school, she always got a very full answer, beginning with who did what to whom in the playground before school, and ending with details of the story his teacher had told at the end of the afternoon. Lizzie did not tell her mum very much because she never asked.

Empathy and justice

One story had a particular effect on Lee. It was 11 November and his teacher had told a story of a young man of only seventeen years old who had been killed rescuing a wounded comrade in the First World War. The incident had touched Lee deeply (he did not know why). It was not because of the excitement and thrill of a war story – there hadn't really been any of that in the way the teacher had told it. It was more a question of empathy. Lee found himself imagining what it must have felt like on the battlefield, frightened but hearing the cries of a wounded friend. Then the dash into 'no man's land' to try and drag him back to the trench. The sense of relief when the man was back – but then the fatal shot!

It was not just that Lee could *imagine* the story: it was more than that. He could begin to *feel* as the heroic soldier had felt. He could begin to *identify* with him.

Although, of course, he didn't realize it, Lee was exhibiting a capacity which becomes increasingly noticeable in the junior child – the ability to see things from another person's perspective. Lee felt for the soldier because he could take the dead man's perspective. He could imagine the feelings of fear, loyalty and love for a friend, which the man had experienced. In a particularly poignant way, the story brought out what was latent in Lee as in other children of his age and development.

Prior to this, as we have seen, infant and early junior children view events from an egocentric standpoint. They see the world out of their own self-centredness. To say this is not to pass a moral judgment: it is to describe the way young children function. They are literally not capable of taking a wider perspective. The world still centres on them as individuals and they can see it in no other terms. With the intellectual and emotional development of juniorhood, this expands into the capacity for empathy which in later years will, if developed, blossom into a sense of justice.

Despite the intellectual, emotional and psychological changes in this period, what stands out is that in their way of understanding, both Lee and Lizzie, irrespective of intelligence, remain rooted in 'concreteness'. This does not mean that they have stood in a bucket of cement, but that they do not yet think in abstract concepts. They still look at matters in terms of the everyday, concrete experience.

This was brought home to Lizzie's student teacher one day during Lizzie's third year. The teacher had been speaking of the injustices of the world. 'Injustice is a wicked thing,' she told the class. 'We must all fight to get rid of it.'

This rallying call, which would have been fine addressed to a teenager, unfortunately meant nothing to these ten year olds, as was evident from the silence when the teacher asked for examples. There was embarrassment as child after child said nothing, or passed with the words 'Don't know'. In the end, Lizzie piped up: 'You mean like serving out school dinners fairly, Miss?' In a few words, Lizzie had captured everything the student had meant but had been unable to communicate to the class. What Lizzie had done was to translate the abstract concept of justice into concrete terms intelligible to her classmates. Most of them were still stuck in the literal, concrete stage. There was no guarantee Lizzie could repeat her triumph but the point had been made and her student teacher was careful not to talk in abstractions again.

New loyalties
Another area in which both Lee and Lizzie (Wendy, too, for that matter) changed considerably in these years was that of group relationships. At infant school, the typical pattern had been for each child to act solely as an individual, even when part of a group. Team games, such as they were, had consisted not so much of a closely-bound team playing for team success as a collection of individuals playing as if they were separate. The notion of group loyalty and activity was non-existent. In the

middle of a game, the infant child would just as likely wander off on his own as get ready to play for the team.

As the junior years passed this changed. Although still an individual, each child learned to act as part of a group. At playtime, they would go around in groups, each with its own identity. On games afternoons, woe betide the player who let the team down! After school, the older children would play out in the street in gangs. The practice of isolated individualism slowly gave way to social cooperation.

An incident in class one day demonstrated this very clearly. Lee's table had been slow in clearing up after art. As the time for lunch approached, Lee spilt a jar of water all over the floor and over Vicki's dress. Vicki hit him and a fight broke out. The teacher, who had been at the other side of the room when it all began, rushed back to find a girl with a soaking dress and a boy with a heavily scratched arm. Vicki's nails had drawn blood.

No amount of questioning could make the group tell on who had been involved. So they all stayed in throughout lunchtime and again the next day. Both Lee and Vicki were grateful for the loyalty of the group and would have done the same in return. But what was striking was the way in which nobody gave them away: to have done so would have been regarded as 'sneaking' and would have forfeited the trust and acceptance of the group.

Such a situation would have been unthinkable five years earlier. No infant would have kept quiet about the culprits. Neither would he have been rejected as a sneak if he had told on them. But by the third year at junior school, the notion of group cooperation and solidarity had become all-powerful. The self-centred world of the infant and early junior had been replaced by the social world of the top junior, with its network of group obligations and codes.

As we have seen, the junior years bring enormous changes in the intellectual, emotional and social development of a child.

Intellectually, we have noticed:
- a thirst for knowledge and information.
- a realization of cause and effect.
- a redefinition of what counts as 'real'.

- an adjustment of infant make-believe.
- a recognition of the difference between reality and fantasy.
- an ordering of events in coherent narrative form.
- an interpretation of everything literally and concretely.

Emotionally, we can see:
- a growing capacity to take the perspective of others.
- a sensitivity towards the feelings of others.
- a reduction in seeing oneself at the centre of the world.

Socially, the child increasingly:
- finds his identity in groups of other children.
- learns to work and play as part of a group.
- develops an overriding loyalty to the group.

The effect on faith development

What effect will these changes have upon a child's development of faith? How do they relate to evangelism? It is time to return to our three-fold definition of faith as believing, trusting and doing. Because of the emphasis among many Christians on faith as believing, we shall focus in some detail upon this first.

1. Believing
In the infant phase, the believing dimension of faith is barely visible. But the rapid growth in the desire and capacity for absorbing knowledge in the junior phase means that the intellectual component of faith becomes much more prominent. The child's natural curiosity about the world in general extends to religion, especially if the child is confronted with believing adults or other children. She will want to know *what* her friend believes, though she may not yet be bothered about the *why*.

The content of Christian belief, however, may pose a major problem. On one hand, as we have noted, the child from seven to ten years is still fascinated by story. This gives the Christian evangelist or teacher a head start, as the gospel is the story of God's involvement with man. But on the other hand, the child is now able to sort out factual stories from fantasy. Into which category will he put the Gospels?

The answer will not be straightforward. It will almost certainly vary from child to child. But the chances are that unless the adults or children he respects believe in the authenticity of scripture, the child will increasingly come to perceive the Gospel stories, especially the miracles and the resurrection, as mythical. A more sophisticated child may say that the Gospel writers got it wrong in their recording of events. But in an age such as our own, where the notion of *revelation* is meaningless to most people, it is more likely that the Bible will simply be written off or ignored.

We should not be surprised at this. After all, the definition of what counts as 'real' for the junior child turns heavily upon what can be observed and experienced by the senses. The junior child faced by stories of Jesus healing blind men, calming the elements, and eventually rising from death, is therefore faced with a massive difficulty – does he believe these things actually happened or does he not? The task is not made easier by the absence of miracles from everyday life. But the conflict is heightened even further if on one hand the storyteller himself clearly believes in these events but on the other hand most of the world clearly does not. This puts to the test the child's acceptance of the authority and wisdom of adults. In the first half of juniorhood, the authority of the adult is still likely to win. Adults are still presumed to know everything and their word is accepted as true. But as the child reaches ten or eleven, this intrinsic authority diminishes. 'Oh, that's only what Mr X or Miss Y believes', becomes the reaction of the older child. The implication is that there are now areas in which the content of what even a respected adult says must be sifted.

Miracles and fantasy

One way in which many children (and adults too!) cope is by a process of compartmentalization: Christian belief is consigned to a specific place or time, such as Sunday school, or it is put into a separate mental compartment which is sealed off from all the others. For example, a child may happily accept the 'scientific' assumption that miracles do not happen and cannot happen now and yet, at the same time, carry on believing that in the time of Jesus they did. Here, he has relegated miracles to history where they are safe from scientific scepticism. No one can travel back in time to check, and so we can give the Gospels the benefit of the doubt. This enables us both to have our miraculous cake and eat it.

Or the child may simply live as if his life is divided into separate worlds in which it is appropriate to believe different things according to whichever world he happens to be moving in at any given moment. So the world of church and Sunday school becomes the place where believing in miracles and Jesus goes on. But when it comes to school or play, no such belief is necessary. Life is divided into boxes each of which has its own set of rules or beliefs. Provided they do not overlap, it does not matter if they are inconsistent with one another. There is no need for a *coherent* view of reality: what matters is that each compartment is consistent within itself and that the whole process works.

The evangelist frequently finds himself faced with a choice. He can either *take no account of child development* and carry on with miracle stories regardless, or he can *shift the emphasis of his message* away from the miraculous.

If he follows the first course, he may justify it by saying that the work of the Spirit in bringing children to faith makes it unnecessary to pay attention to theories of child development. But this would be both theologically and practically naive. We now know enough about the growth and development of children to be able to describe the processes involved and, as Christians, we would maintain that this is how God, in his wisdom, has structured their development. The evangelist or teacher who refuses to recognize and respect this is like a gardener who refuses to test the soil and sows plants which cannot grow. When they die he does not question his method, he simply blames the soil or the plants. The Christian worker who refuses to take account of the multiple ways in which children develop needs to ask himself whether he is any wiser than such a gardener.

If he follows the second course, shifting the emphasis of his message away from the miraculous, he need not end up ignoring miracles altogether. He should, instead, be clear about what he *does* wish to emphasize. Jesus, significantly, was sparing in his use of miracles and did not use them in order to impress his audience or convince them of his overwhelming power. He used them as signs to point to God's active purpose in the world establishing his kingdom. He also, of course, acted miraculously out of compassion.

This brings us to the nub of the problem. Given the likelihood that children will always tend to see miracle stories in terms of magic, can we use them creatively, not so much to try to recreate the sense of astonishment and wonder felt by the original observers, as to convey the truth that the same Christ who performed these marvellous acts is the Jesus who today calls us to be his friends?

This refocussing moves the hearer away from concentration on the 'magical' aspect of the miracles to what, after all, is the core of the gospel message: that God acts out of love on behalf of people in need. The cross and the resurrection are the greatest miracles of all.

By emphasizing the miracles as acts of love, the evangelist or teacher is thus able to speak openly and with integrity about the reality of miracles without encouraging children's preoccupation with the magical. He can recount the Gospel accounts without reducing them to mere acts of wizardry. Moreover, he can speak of them as historical events: they represent specific occasions on which God demonstrated how much he loved ordinary human beings who otherwise were helpless.

Used wisely, then, the miracle stories of the New Testament can enlarge a child's understanding of Jesus. Used unwisely, however, they may simply reinforce notions of magic which, in later years, will be discarded as infantile along with stories of pumpkins turning into stagecoaches and frogs into princes.

Christian teaching and literal understanding

If the miracles pose a problem for a child's sense of fantasy, the abstract nature of Christian teaching poses problems for his sense of literalness. The junior child thinks in concrete, literal terms. This requires us rigorously to examine our teaching in two areas.

Firstly, *we must be careful about the use of figurative language*. Phrases such as 'Take Jesus into your heart', or 'Jesus is knocking at the door of your heart' will conjure up pictures of him actually opening a little door inside our bodies. Likewise, talk of Jesus 'living inside us' will be equally misleading. I have heard children ask, after an evangelistic message based on this kind of language, in exactly which part of the human body Jesus makes his home.

It is a salutary exercise to spend time going through an evangelistic talk in advance, weeding out the metaphors that will be misunderstood (which will be just about every one). Remember, a child up to about ten and a half or eleven will interpret words literally. If in doubt, find a different way to make the same point. Here are some examples:

The metaphor:	Will be taken to mean:	So should be rephrased:
Let Jesus into your heart.	Open up your chest.	Take Jesus as your close friend.
Taste and see the Lord is good.	God can be eaten like food.	When we know God as a friend, we will find out how wonderful he is.
You must be born again.	You must get back into your mother's tummy.	(Best left alone).

Secondly, *we must work at turning abstract concepts into concrete teaching*. The notions of sin and redemption, for example, presuppose an essentially adult ability to comprehend abstract truth. The only remedy for this is to translate the ideas behind them into *examples* which are intelligible to the literalistic mind.

This is not just a matter of using shorter words. Nothing could be shorter than the word 'sin'. But, as John Inchley has pointed out, the term creates enormous confusion even among adults. It is far better to speak of 'wrongdoing', which is familiar and denotes a recognizable experience.[1] In this way the idea is retained but without the abstract language.

The most concrete experiences for children are those which involve day-to-day relationships. To cast the gospel in terms of a relationship, therefore, cashes in on the most powerful experiences in a child's life. It also, as we have seen, chimes with a growing awareness of the perspective of other people. To portray sin as the breaking of friendship with God and the death of Jesus as God's way of restoring that friendship can evoke powerful feelings as a child puts himself in the place of God or of his Son.

Our purpose must not be to manipulate children's emotions but to enable them to get inside the skin of the gospel. A skilful presentation in terms which encourage the child to imagine how God or Jesus felt when faced with human sin will go much further than simply laying out the 'ABC' of evangelism or the four steps to salvation.

Believing at the junior age, then, is a very complex business. The evangelist who does not recognize the developmental characteristics of the phase will either end up with children committing themselves to a message they have not understood, because they want to please; or with children who seem to accept what is said but whose capacity for future scepticism has been significantly increased.

2. Trusting

We have seen that trusting is the foremost feature of faith in infancy. Although this is overtaken by intellectual belief during the junior years, the patterns of covenantal trust established in infancy continue to provide the emotional framework for faith.

So it is that Lee can cope more readily than Lizzie with the intellectual challenges of the junior years, because he is more secure when faced with new knowledge that threatens his previous understanding. He is also more able to trust the adults who impart such knowledge.

For Lizzie, however, the absence from babyhood of a love bond between herself and her mother makes it more difficult for her to handle new information or new ways of looking at things. It is much harder to launch out into uncharted waters if no one has ever taught you to swim or if you have never been able to trust anyone to do so. This is Lizzie's position when her previously uncritical ideas about God and Jesus come under threat from her classmates or her own discovery of the material world of cause and effect.

Faced with this crisis, Lizzie can do several things: she can continue to believe in her infant-based notions of God, so that the developments in her general intellectual capacities are cut off from the area of faith; she can give up her previous beliefs completely; she can substitute faith in a person (probably an adult such as Wendy's mum) for faith in God. Or she can muddle along with a mixture of all three as she goes through the same developmental struggle and growth as other children. There is no way of predicting exactly which course the Lizzies of this world will follow: we can only be aware of the problems and possibilities.

For example, if she separates her intellectual capacities from her infant-based notion of God, Lizzie might simply lap up all we say, even at the late junior stage (when we would expect her to be asking more critical questions). Or, if she substitutes faith in the evangelist for faith in God, she may sidestep the challenge of our message ('Oh yes, I believe all that') in order to fawn upon the evangelist in unswerving obedience and loyalty. Alternatively she may, for the same reason, make an overt and apparently enthusiastic commitment. Or she may be totally unable to make any emotional commitment at all since this would involve an act of trust which is beyond her capability.

Of course, not every child who exhibits one or other of these features is a Lizzie. All children are like this to some degree. But we do well to remember that children's reactions to evangelistic teaching are notoriously easy to misread. The evangelist who gets a hundred hands raised in response to an appeal will need to discern with care and wisdom what kind of processes have been at work. For it is very difficult to trust an invisible God at an age when the real world is defined as what can be seen, felt, touched and spoken to. Indeed, it is hard to know what *is* going on in a junior child who professes to trust in Christ. While we must not rule out the possibility of a work of faith similar to that experienced by adults, we must recognize that a more complex process is almost certainly at work – a process which will involve, on the child's part, an element of faith *in the evangelist* or teacher. He, after all, is the visible, tangible representative of the invisible Christ. And, moreover, he can enter into a face-to-face relationship with the child. Given the literalness and concreteness of children's thinking, it would be surprising if this element were not large. We shall look at this again when we come to discuss conversion.

3. Doing

The junior child is unbelievably *active* and eager to please. Many a parent will have reached the point of exhaustion while their children are still going strong, showing no sign of tiring. A child's understanding of faith as doing, is, therefore, a natural extension of this characteristic. Again, because of the concreteness of understanding at this age, children cannot draw any distinction between faith and works. Doing is bound up with being, and cannot be otherwise.

Perhaps in this they are more biblical than adults. By perceiving faith in Jesus as a relationship, children automatically assume that this involves doing things. The notion of a faith which is purely reflective and which does not issue in activity is literally inconceivable. Although it might be possible to have activity without faith, the converse could not be true. You might as well try to imagine water that isn't wet.

So the evangelist who majors on 'learning by doing' is making a choice which is not only educationally but theologically sound. The evangelist or Sunday school teacher who expects passive absorption of ideas by a crowd of docile youngsters will get neither passivity nor absorption. This is especially important to remember in using story as a teaching medium, for it is often perceived as passive. In fact, good storytelling is highly active. It will involve both the teller and the hearers through their emotions, imagination and, in some cases, the acting out of parts of the story itself.

Yet it is surprising how many children's workers still believe that the most effective form of communication remains the set-piece talk. This is a complete misapprehension. While the talk may achieve something if it forms part of a total package with plenty of activities, the talk itself will, in terms of learning, achieve only a limited amount. The adage is true; children take in:

10% of what they hear
50% of what they see
60% of what they say
90% of what they do.

The implication is clear: we must rely less on talking *at* children and more on working, and being, *with* them.

The shift in focus

If faith during infancy is a matter of trusting with instinctive feelings, faith in juniorhood is a matter of believing with the developing intellect. With the junior phase, we have majored on the educational characteristics of the child since it is in this area that great strides are made. No less important, however, is that the focus of a child's existence shifts away from the relatively narrow boundaries of home to the expanding horizons of the wider world. School is especially important in this broadening process as the child becomes less and less dependent upon parents and family for knowledge, and more and more dependent upon teachers and classmates.

It is at school that the child is exposed to a cluster of differing or even conflicting beliefs which challenge the world in which he has grown up. In contemporary society, Christianity is simply one among many views in the marketplace of belief. The evangelist can no longer presume prior Christian understanding or knowledge of even a rudimentary kind. Although the term 'secularization' is unthinkingly and often inaccurately used to describe what has happened in Britain over the last twenty-five years, it is nevertheless true that Christianity must now fight as hard as any other set of beliefs to gain a hearing or to win adherents.

This hotchpotch of beliefs makes it imperative that evangelists and children's workers understand the mental, emotional and social world in which our children operate. An appreciation of the process of child development during the crucial junior years is therefore especially important.

Taking spiritual stock

Experienced faith

It is now time to take stock of the spiritual side of Lee and Lizzie's development. The infant and junior years belong to what John Westerhoff III has called the period of *experienced faith*.[2] It is the time when patterns of believing, trusting and doing are the product of what is learned from others. This may take the form of negative as well as positive learning, but it is learning nonetheless. In this, as we have seen, the models provided by home, school, media and community are crucial.

A secular belief system
For both Lee and Lizzie, as for the majority of children in Britain, the models with which they have been confronted have been far from distinctively *Christian*. They have been based on an underlying indifference towards the Christian faith, except as the source of moral teaching or of inspirational examples. And they have refused (if they ever understood) any kind of commitment to Christ as the risen, living Lord.

We need to be careful at this point. It is not that the average parent or family deliberately rejects God. It is simply that they do not feel they need him, except in emergencies or times of stress or when they want to mark some life-changing occasion such as birth, marriage or death. If they were presented with God in person, they would bow the knee. But, like the junior child for whom reality is what can be seen, touched or measured, they have never seen, touched or measured God. They do not say he has ceased to exist, or that he is a figment of our imaginations: they simply note that they have never encountered him and, therefore, they had better get on with their lives as best they can. He may be *there* but from the point of view of daily experience he is not *real*.

This is what is generally meant when society is described as secular. It is not that everyone has ceased to believe in God but that Christian truth and Christian symbols have ceased to be the means by which most people order their lives or make sense of existence. The acquisition of material goods, or the pursuit of social justice (or some other ideal), or the Welfare State have come to do the job instead.

So it is that children from non-Christian homes may not necessarily be opposed to Christian faith, but neither do they find the patterns of their lives shaped by it. As they grow older, it is not likely to be the Christian minister to whom they turn in times of trouble but the local GP.

Westerhoff's period of 'experienced faith', then, will be very patchy. The faith acquired will be closer to Fowler's definition of faith as a system of meanings than to a biblically-oriented Christianity.

So what might the evangelist expect to find in the 'experienced faith' outlook of Lee or Lizzie?

In neither Lee's nor Lizzie's case was Christian faith a significant factor in the outlook of their parents. Christianity was not important in enabling them to give meaning to their lives. They did not consciously draw upon it as a way of making sense of the world. If it had any relevance at all, it was in the realm of morality: 'do good to others, love your neighbour.' But even here it rarely became more practical than an unattainable ideal.

Relationships in the home
What was equally significant, however, for the development of Lee's and Lizzie's experience was the *quality* of relationships and values experienced by them in their early years. This gave a context for the system of beliefs which their parents held.

In Lizzie's case, the experience of rejection formed the bedrock of how she came to understand herself, her family and her world. Only with the advent of Wendy and her family did this begin to erode as an alternative value – love – was shown. For Lee, love was part and parcel of life from the beginning. His understanding of himself and the world, therefore, was much better adjusted.

In teenage years, this could prove decisive. It is here that the struggle to find identity rages. A child like Lizzie who has experienced little parental love will find it hard to believe in a God who is Father and who claims to love us as his children. It will not be much good saying to Lizzie, 'God loves you as much as your parents love you.' For she has a chronic distrust of parents and has experienced only suffering at their hands. If Lee, on the other hand, is to come to faith in Christ at all, it will be the security of his relationship with his parents which, on the human side, paves the way. For Lizzie, her best hope lies in her substitute relationship with Wendy's parents. This may have been powerful enough to give her sufficiently positive feelings towards adults and therefore towards God who is (unconsciously if not consciously) conceived of as a super-adult.

The examples of Lee and Lizzie point to a common but

important paradox. On one hand, children from loving and accepting non-Christian homes may well come to a robust faith in Christ upon hearing the gospel, for they have experienced from birth what it means to be loved and to trust even though they have not been exposed to Christian teaching. On the other hand, children who have experienced rejection (even in a nominally Christian home) may have immense difficulties in entering into or sustaining a deep faith because, while they may know the content of belief, they have not experienced human love which paves the way for accepting God's love.

'School' Christianity

A third factor common to our fictional pair, as to most children, is that the bulk of their understanding of the Christian faith has come through school. They do not attend Sunday school and their homes have not seen Christianity as relevant, so what they have learned has been passed on by teachers. This has meant that Lee and Lizzie have probably received a very inadequate understanding of faith in Christ, amounting to little more than a collection of Bible stories and woolly inspiration. They are unlikely to have any idea of the core of Christian belief.

But, more importantly, they have encountered even this watered-down version of Christian faith in a purely *educational* context, which is essentially secular. If, however, one truth stands out from scripture and the life of the church, it is that faith in all its meanings, makes sense only in the context of worship. We often forget that the first Christians formulated what they believed and how they should live (faith as believing and doing) as an act of worship. They did not sit down and write out systematic works of theology – that came later. They first encountered Christ, worshipped him and then worked out what it meant to live as a Christian.

For Lee and Lizzie, this crucial dimension is missing. They know only *about* Jesus. They do not know his presence in the community of faithful worshippers. The school cannot be expected to fulfil this role. Teachers are not trained or equipped to lead Christian worship and the days of a regular assembly which incorporated Christian acts of worship are numbered, if not gone.

CONCLUSION

The task of the evangelist or children's worker, then, is much more complex than simply delivering a gospel talk. He will have to pick up, and make good, the deficiencies of understanding and experience which are the lot of many children today. Ideally, he will need to recognize what stage of development of faith a child or group of children has reached and shape the message and its context accordingly. For the travelling evangelist this will not be easy and he will rely upon detailed information and assessment from local people who know their situation well. This will require careful liaison and planning and above all a local team who are familiar with faith development and who know how to read the situation. The regular children's worker or Sunday school teacher, of course, is in a different position. He or she will already know his or her children and, provided there is a willingness and openness to the task of analysis, can set objectives specific to them. Although such work and research may seem complicated and burdensome, it is the only way to develop an effective ministry that is both true to the gospel and true to the ways in which the Holy Spirit may be using the processes of child development to create an appropriate response of faith.

NOTES TO CHAPTER 3

1. John Inchley, *All About Children*, Eastbourne: Coverdale, 1976, pp 89–90. See also John Inchley, *Realities of Childhood*, London: Scripture Union 1986, pp 122–123.
2. John Westerhoff III, *Will Our Children Have Faith?* New York, Seabury Press 1976, pp 94–96.

4
Adolescence

The 'crisis' of adolescence:

The years of change
  Physical change
  Appearance
  Friendship groups
  Rows and questions
The struggle for identity
  Self discovery
  Ability to reflect

The interrelation of faith development, evangelism and conversion:

Evangelistic implications
  Affiliative faith
  The evangelist's reaction
  Evaluating response
When does faith development end?
Further faith developments
  Searching faith
  Owned faith

The years of change

The move to comprehensive school was unlike anything Lee and Lizzie had ever experienced. Whereas they had been in a school of 200, they were now among 1700. Whereas they had been top dogs as fourth-year juniors, they were now lowly first-years of whom nobody took much notice. Whereas they had known every teacher in their last school, they now didn't even *see* half of them. The headmaster was a distant figure, known only as 'Old Munby' who appeared once a week at lower school assembly. The rest of the time, you saw either your head of year or, in the worst cases, the head of lower school. In neither instance was the visit likely to be a pleasure.

In the first two years, Lee and Lizzie's development carried on much as before. In many ways, they were larger versions of juniorhood. But under the surface, major changes were beginning to take place.

Physical change

As they reached the end of the second year it became obvious that, like their companions, they were moving into adolescence. Physically, the transition from child to adult was under way. As soon as this began, Lee's parents introduced him to the facts of life in liaison with the school's programme of sex education. In this way, they were able to make progress together. As usual, however, Lizzie's parents were untroubled. Her mother gave her a booklet and a talking to but beyond that there was no further communication. Fortunately, Wendy's mum had anticipated this and took Lizzie under her wing.

But the physical changes were the least of anybody's difficulties. The 'stormy tunnel of adolescence' had been entered.

Appearance

For Lizzie, this showed itself in an obsession with her appearance. She would spend hours in front of a mirror, checking out that she had the right clothes, make-up and hairstyle. Her mother got tired of it but could do nothing. At first, Lizzie would ask her if she looked all right: it was as if she needed her mother's approval. But since her mother soon made it clear she resented being bothered, Lizzie gradually stopped asking.

Lee's awakening to appearance came later, but when it arrived it was no less fierce. It started with the constant checking and combing of hair. But it quickly progressed to being concerned about all aspects of his appearance. To his parents' surprise, Lee became fashion-conscious and would spend his clothing allowance (£50 every three months) on the latest jumpers, jackets and shoes. He did not quite become a peacock, but he did become highly sensitive to what people might think of him.

Friendship groups

At the same time, both youngsters (they could hardly be called children any more) attached themselves to specific groups or gangs of 'mates' with whom they went around most of the time. This had begun to happen in earlier years, but now it took a much more distinctive shape.

The difference lay in the extent to which each group of friends now claimed the loyalty of its members above all other loyalties. The incident in junior school with Vicki had revealed the beginning of this process, but by the age of thirteen Lee and Lizzie, in common with everyone else, found their identities no longer in home or school but in relation to their friends.

Previously their friends had provided only one among many competing centres of interest and influence, but now they were predominant. What the gang believed, each member believed. What the gang did, each member did. Parents and school had to struggle to get a toe in at all.

The most amusing example of this had been over the question of ear-rings. The school allowed neither boys nor girls to wear them. But one day, Shaun, a member of Lee's circle, arrived sporting a ring in his left ear. He was told to remove it, whereupon he found it promptly confiscated. The next day Shaun reappeared with another ring. However, it had become not only Shaun this time, but half the class. By the end of the week, Mr Simmons the class teacher had over fifty rings in his drawer. As he put it to his colleagues in the staff room, 'The herd instinct has taken over again from school rules or common sense.'

The same applied to questions of belief. When one person in the class announced she was turning to astrology, so did everyone else. For two weeks, the only topic of conversation was horoscopes and astral signs. If you did not know your birth sign or did not believe the horoscope you were definitely out in the cold.

This intensity of belonging to a group meant that in just about every matter of significance, it was the group's view that counted. The views of teachers or parents were all subsidiary. In any clash, it was always the group which won the loyalty of its members.

Rows and questions

At home this led to enormous rows. Lizzie, who by this time had come to reject her parents intensely, clashed with her mother on several occasions. It was on one of these that her mother shouted that she wished Lizzie had never been born. Lizzie screamed back that she had not asked to be brought into the world and at this her mother withdrew her harsh words. But, inwardly, Lizzie knew that they had only given voice to what they had both felt for years. The rejection she had felt from birth had been brought out into the open. It was never to be healed.

Lee, meanwhile, had begun to question just about everything his parents believed in or stood for. He no longer wanted to do things as part of the family. He did not want to identify with the community association of which they were members (he had always enjoyed their social events in the past). And he did not want to go on holiday with them. He wanted more freedom of choice in what he wore, how he looked and when he was to come in at night. In short, he became the typical rebellious teenager.

At school, both Lee and Lizzie fitted into the system but were careful to distance themselves from it. Like most of their friends, they were decidedly 'stand-offish' towards it.

There was, however, one exception to this for each of them. Lizzie did not care for most teachers (they were part of 'the system') but she did like Mrs Hampton, her English teacher. This was largely because she allowed Lizzie the freedom to escape. Lizzie had always liked stories and, even at junior school, had used them as a means of escape. Now, with things becoming worse at home, Lizzie found relief in literature. Mrs Hampton realized this and sympathized. Moreover, when it came to setting study projects for homework, she would agree to Lizzie's request not to study books with a plot majoring on family life: it was simply too painful.

As a result, Lizzie liked and respected her. Her homework was always in on time and well presented. Its quality was high too. The approval she sought from home and which was not forthcoming (her parents never came to open evenings at the school), Lizzie now found in a combination of Mrs Hampton and Wendy's mum and dad, who more than ever had become surrogate parents.

Lee likewise found an alternative parent in the person of Mr Payne the sports master. At first sight, this seemed a bit strange since Lee hated sport. He was no good at it and would do anything to get out of games periods, including falsifying sickness notes and feigning illness. Mr Payne, however, saw through all this. But he would have none of it. One afternoon, while the class were out on a cross country run, he took Lee to one side and found out what the problem was. It had happened that as a child, Lee had needed an operation on his leg. This left him with a poor sense of balance and coordination. It had also left an unsightly scar. On both counts Lee was deeply embarrassed in front of the class. He always had been, but it was worse now.

Mr Payne's remedy was to give Lee some special training sessions after school and a schedule of exercises for use at home. Within a matter of weeks, the combination of personal attention and proper training had developed skills Lee never dreamt he had. He would not become the star of the school football team, but he learned to play a decent game and was selected to play for his house.

One result was that although the rebellious streak remained, Lee became much more settled. At home he rejoined family activities and even volunteered to run a stall at the community association's summer fete. His parents heaved a sigh of relief and hoped that the peak of teenage turbulence had passed.

The struggle for identity

This brief sketch of the early years of adolescence carries us to the limit of our study. By their mid-teens, Lee, Lizzie and the thousands like them can hardly be called children. And yet in vital ways they are. The teenage years bring discontinuity with what has gone before, but they also reveal a considerable amount of continuity. Teenagers do not suddenly cease to be all that they have been previously. Adolescence builds on the experiences of childhood: it does not erase them.

But, as any parent will know, adolescence introduces developments and problems which are of a different order from those of childhood. The biggest of these is the *struggle for identity*. James Fowler has described puberty as a time of mirrors.[1] The teenager is constantly preoccupied with his image. This takes its most obvious form in an incessant concern for how he *looks*: 'Is my hair all right? Does this jacket fit? Is it fashionable? Do my spots show?' The sensitivity of a teenager to what will later seem trivia is unbounded.

Self discovery

The outward, however, is only half the story. It is the *inward* struggle for identity which acts as the driving force behind the anxieties that beset these years. This in itself is part of the process of mirroring. For at the same time as the adolescent asks whether his outward appearance is acceptable, he is also asking what others think of him as a *person*. He is not only trying to find out how he looks: he wants to know whether others like him. As Fowler puts it: 'He or she needs the eyes and ears of a few trusted others in which to see the image of personality emerging.'

This attempt by the teenager to construct or find an identity combines with the hormonal and other physical changes which accompany puberty. Together these forces create the inner turbulence and even violence experienced from twelve or thirteen years onwards. For the first time in his life, the teenager is confronted with the question, 'Who am I?' Both his physical and his mental growth tell him that he is growing up fast. But for what? And into what? It is a frightening time as each day brings new changes in body and mood, both of which seem uncontrollable. In all of this the experiences of the past will be influencing the processes of the present, as he or she struggles to create a new identity out of the old.

Models of adolescence

There are two ways of looking at this teenage identity crisis, though the one does not exclude aspects of the other. The first sees adolescence as an *explosion*. This is apt in many ways because the characteristics of an explosion – its force, its potential for destruction, its raw power – are precisely those which are present in puberty.

Yet even here we must draw a distinction. For there are controlled as well as uncontrolled explosions. The identity crisis of the teenage years is not always unpredictable or destructive. For instance, it is predictable in that we know everyone experiences it in generally similar ways. And it can usually be contained, provided that wise parents and others know what is going on and so build in safety valves. It may be explosive but it does not have to destroy everything in its path.

The second way of looking at puberty is to compare it to a *chrysalis*. This may seem too gentle given that we have already likened it to an explosion. But the comparison is nevertheless valid. It conveys the ideas of transition, growth and emergence – the features of the chrysalis as it moves from being a caterpillar to becoming a butterfly – and the characteristics of teenhood. The boy or girl who enters puberty in the second or third year of comprehensive school is not the same boy or girl who emerges from it in the fifth or sixth form.

This process of self-discovery is always painful. But it is doubly so if we have never been sure of those who gave us selfhood in the first place. This is why Lizzie found it so difficult. Prior to adolescence, her identity had been formed for her by a combination of relationships given to her *'from the outside'* – her family, her class at school, her gang of friends and so on. But now she is discovering an identity that springs *from within* as she begins to ask herself questions about meaning and purpose.

In this situation, our feelings assure us that there is meaning and purpose to our existence because we sense that we have been valued in our own right from the beginning of our lives. We would not have been born otherwise. We are here because someone wanted us to be here and therefore our lives began with a loving purpose. For Lizzie and children like her, however, her deepest feelings tell her nothing of the kind. If they tell her anything it is that she has never been wanted by those who brought her into the world. For her there are no memories of soft words and cuddles to reassure her that there is meaning and purpose, and that she is loved.

It is at this point that the covenantal love of babyhood once again becomes crucial. Lizzie is not as desperate as some because she has found an alternative source of warmth and care in Wendy's family. But even these will not completely erase the pain of rejection by those who were responsible for her entry into the world (a decision over which she had no control and for which she has suffered ever since).

Ability to reflect

A second factor in the search for identity is the new-found ability of the teenager to reflect. We noted earlier that the junior child is able to order his thoughts and experience in narrative form but that he always operates from within the stream of the story. ('I did this, then we did that' and so on). But with adolescence comes the ability to stand back from the flow and reflect upon it. We can compare these two stages to a stream. The junior is always *in* the stream. Even when he is recounting what goes on, he is doing so while standing in the middle of it. He cannot look at it from any other standpoint. The teenager, however, is able to stand on the bank and comment on what is happening even when he remains part of the flow. It is as if he has developed the capacity to observe himself through the eyes of a spectator.

This is what 'the time of mirrors' means. The teenager standing on the bank is worried about what others may think of him as they, too, stand on the bank. He is continually anxious about his image.

The 'others' who matter, however, are no longer those who mattered during childhood. Parents must take a back seat. Those whose opinions are sought are increasingly the teenager's friends. It is his contemporaries whom he wants to impress, not his elders.

The incident with the ear-rings was a classic example of this, as were the 'herd' reactions to astrology and sporting ability. Lee's loathing of sport was not just a question of embarrassment about his scar (after all, he had played games at junior school) but resulted from a keen awareness that the majority were good at sport while he wasn't. It was better not to take part than to look a fool, even if this meant deception.

Emotions and physique, however, are not all there is to puberty. In earlier stages of development we noticed intellectual changes too. Is there a corresponding shift in teenage years?

The answer is yes, but not in the same way. The key development in teenage understanding is the ability to move from concrete to abstract thinking. For example, at junior school Lizzie translated the abstract concept of justice into concrete terms of school dinners. Now she would be able to reverse the procedure. Faced with a specific situation, she would be able to say whether or not it was just, according to how well it conformed to an abstract notion of justice.

This shift in mental ability is frequently uneven and patchy. Not all adolescents reach the same level of abstraction. Some move only a little way beyond the concrete stage. And it is a fact that vast numbers of adults remain stuck in early adolescence for most of their lives. Hence the popularity of tabloid newspapers written entirely around concrete ways of thinking.

Emotionally and intellectually, therefore, teenagers undergo nothing short of a revolution. What implications does this have for evangelism?

Evangelistic implications

Affiliative faith

In contrast to the period of 'experienced faith' which marked the infant and junior years, the adolescent moves into what Westerhoff has called *affiliative faith*.[2] This is marked by three features.

Identifying with the faith of friends

Firstly, the teenager joins himself to, and identifies with, the faith of his friends. This may not be Christian faith at all. It may be trivial astrology, agnosticism, pleasure-seeking or whatever. Or, if his friends are mainly Christians, it may be Christianity. The fact is that he will identify with what his friends accept rather than find an individually thought-out faith for himself. It is the herd instinct at work.

Dominance of feelings

The second feature of affiliative faith is found in the dominance of feelings and affections. In the swirl of emotions and changing perceptions, feelings come to control everything. It is what feels OK that counts, irrespective of intellectual coherence or integrity.

Questioning authority

Thirdly, there is the question of authority. This no longer resides in adults or institutions, pure and simple. Authority, religious or otherwise, must win its spurs. It must gain the right to be heard and obeyed by submitting itself to inspection. If it does not conform to the teenager's sense of values or priorities, it will not be accepted as worthwhile. An authority – that of the school, for instance – may enforce *acceptance* by virtue of its power; but it will not win the *allegiance* of the adolescent who does not agree that its rule is valid. The most it can do is hope to enforce conformity.

The stage of affiliative faith, then, is one in which the evangelist will have to fight even to get a hearing. We all know the youth club syndrome where teenagers happily give themselves to recreational activities but switch off during the epilogue. The 'God slot' becomes the price to pay for having somewhere to meet as a group.

The evangelist's reaction

How should we react to this? In the end it boils down to two alternatives: we can either try to undermine the affiliative instinct or we can work with it. Many of the problems encountered by workers with this age group arise because of a failure or refusal to acknowledge the importance of the affiliative stage. We try to usher adolescents into individual (essentially adult) ways of thinking and behaviour for which they are not yet ready. That will come in the next stage.

The answer almost certainly is to 'go with the flow': to accept that the thirteen to sixteen year old is going to find his identity in gangs or groups, and construct a programme which reflects this. This will mean becoming a member of the group with all its obligations and loyalties. It is no good trying to be a wolf in sheep's clothing, pretending to be in tune with the affiliations of the group when all along you only want to fit its members into an adult mould.

In practical terms, this will mean working and playing with the group in a relationship of equals. Although the evangelist may *suggest* a structure of activities, say, during a holiday club week, if he is wise he will not *impose* it. He will be ready to accept the overruling of the group provided a constructive alternative is proposed, and he will be very wary about invoking the notion of authority.

In terms of what to teach, much will depend upon the intellectual stage of the group. In the early teens, there is a fine balance to be struck between the concrete and the abstract. In any case, abstract concepts need to be well illustrated even for adults, so it will be better to err on the side of concreteness than abstraction. What is clear, however, is that simply talking *at* teenagers is more often than not counter-productive. Although they may be willing to accept the gospel from someone they like and respect, they will not swallow whole slabs of teaching simply because the evangelist 'says so'.

Evaluating response

The result of all this will be variable. In some cases, there will be no response. In others, we may discover a strong response. But just as we need to exercise wisdom and discernment in evaluating responses made by juniors, so we need to do the same towards teenagers. For an adolescent who seems to make a commitment to Christ may be doing one or a combination of things:

- responding to an adult he has come to like and respect and whom he wants to please;
- following the herd or the example of a friend;
- seeking an answer to his identity crisis;
- trying to discover a new affiliative group to which he can belong;
- seeking Christ as the Spirit leads him into repentance and faith.

None of these can be excluded and most commitments probably include an element of each. The important point is that if we have an understanding of the features of affiliative faith, we shall be better equipped to interpret a teenager's response. If we do not, there is a good chance we shall naively misread the situation and so mishandle it.

More problematically, this means that we have to be prepared to watch teenagers apparently move in and out of faith as their identities and affiliations switch back and forth. When faced with this situation, it is tempting to apply adult categories and chide them for backsliding, or question their sincerity. Although there may be times when this is necessary, the nature of adolescent development means this need not be a permanent state of affairs but can lead on to something more stable and long-lasting. Godly patience and a love of butterflies are perhaps the qualities most to be sought by the Christian worker with teenagers.

When does faith development end?

We have reached the end of Lee and Lizzie's life stories. Or at least, that part which is relevant to this book. They are now sixteen or seventeen and to all intents and purposes have become young adults. In a year or two's time the law will recognize them fully as adults and accord them the right to vote, marry, and fight for their country.

But it is not the end of their development as persons or in faith. How they might develop in either realm would require a book of its own. On any model of growth, they still have a long way to go.

To leave their stories at this point, however, would be to exit at the most crucial time. It would be like getting to the ultimate cliffhanger in a novel – only to discover that the publisher had decided to print no more pages!

What follows in this chapter is not the definitive 'plot' for the rest of Lee and Lizzie's lives, but a sketching of possibilities. Although patterns have emerged in the course of their childhood and adolescence, the exact direction in which these will go cannot be predicted in advance. When we have got as far as models of human and faith development can take us, a number of stages still lie ahead. Moreover, there are many variable choices and possibilities within these stages. Lee and Lizzie may choose one or a combination of them: their choices are not determined in advance.

One distinct possibility has to be borne in mind: they may not go through any further stages of development at all. They may simply travel through life stuck at the stage of development they reached by late teens. This is a common phenomenon; large numbers of adults do not get very far past the concrete thinking stage in intellectual development. This is why political organizations cast their messages in concrete terms. People do not want to discuss the abstract rights and wrongs of large-scale issues: they want to know how they will be affected in their daily lives.

In the same way, it is probably true to say that in religion the majority of the population does not move beyond the affiliative faith stage of early adolescence. Whether we define faith as believing, trusting or doing, the fact is that few people have a faith that amounts to more than the consensus of views held by their companions. It is not quite as crude as the herd instinct but it is not far off.

So we find that in a mass democracy such as Britain or the United States, where the influence of the media is all-pervasive, there are *general* views about Christianity as about everything else. Those who have a carefully worked-out faith for themselves that will stand up when others round about are saying something different are few and far between.

Lee and Lizzie may go through further stages of growth, then, or they may not. In the remainder of this chapter, we shall look at what these might be. For the definitive conclusion to the Lee and Lizzie saga, however, the reader will have to fall back upon his or her own literary talents.

Further faith developments

John Westerhoff has suggested that if there is to be full development of faith a person will go through four stages.[3] Stage 1 is that of *experienced faith*, which, as we have seen, is crucial in babyhood and infancy. Stage 2 is the time of *affiliative faith*, when children (and some adults who never move beyond this stage) believe what their friends or family believe but have not yet come to a thought-out faith for themselves. Stage 3 he describes as *searching faith*, and stage 4 as *owned faith*. We have already observed the characteristics of experienced and affiliative faith. It remains for us to see what is meant by searching and owned faith.

Searching faith

This comes typically in late teens, although it may come as late as the thirties or not at all. Since searching faith and conversion frequently go hand in hand, however, and since the majority of conversions take place in teenage years, we shall locate it earlier rather than later.

As the teenager develops a sense of identity, new questions and doubts crop up. He becomes dissatisfied with previous answers to questions of meaning and purpose. Moreover, he finds that going along with the faith of the crowd is inadequate: he must have his own answers, not somebody else's. He is therefore increasingly driven on by questions across the whole range of life.

James Fowler has pointed out that the person moving into the searching stage is often someone who belongs to a community or group which has a strong sense of identity and beliefs. These may become too rigid or out of touch with the rest of the searcher's experience for him to accept them any longer. A good example of this would be a teenager who grows up in a rigid evangelical home and church but has never experienced anything wider or different. He has made a public profession of faith because that seemed natural. But in fact, his faith is still at the affiliative stage. At some point he encounters other people, beliefs or situations which challenge his upbringing (at university for instance). But because he has only ever moved in circles which have reinforced his beliefs and not questioned them, he does not have the equipment to meet the new challenge. His profession of faith was sincere but it did not develop out of struggle and is not adequate to cope with the questions which now assail him.

This leads to experimentation. Because his previous set of beliefs and values are now unable to supply what he wants, he may dip into a wide variety of philosophies and cultures. The search for truth may lead him into all kinds of practices which he will later come to disown or regret – mysticism, cults, astrology, drugs. At the least, the searcher will explore beyond the bounds of his earlier assumptions as he examines the claims of other religions, politics and lifestyles.

But this searching is not just intellectual. There is an emotional searching as well, a need for commitment to persons and causes: Oxfam, socialism, the poor, liberty, democracy, to mention but a few. The searcher is looking for someone or something to give himself to, which in return will give him meaning and purpose.

We can see how different searching faith is from what has gone before. The searcher is much more conscious of himself as an individual made for meaning and purpose. He is no longer content to live on the surface of life, eating, drinking and making merry. He has moved beyond the point where superficial pleasure for its own sake contains any answers. He must find something which touches the depths of his being.

So far, the searcher has been self-centred. Not in an immoral way but he has been concerned to find truth that will make sense for *him*. Westerhoff now introduces a factor which will turn the searcher away from himself. He calls this the *act of surrender*.

When the searcher surrenders himself to a belief or cause, he acknowledges with his heart and mind that meaning lies outside himself and lays a claim upon him. He is jolted into accepting that he is not the beginning and end of everything and that in order to find true meaning and purpose he must stop acting as if he were. This is the essence of surrender. It leads directly to the fourth stage, *owned faith*.

Owned faith

The act of surrender opens the door to a new way of believing. The light has dawned, the penny has dropped. The world will never be the same again. The searcher has found faith *for himself*: not as one of a crowd, not as the recipient of something handed down but as an individual making a personal discovery that changes his life. In Christian terms, it is the moment of conversion. But we need to note that owned faith does not only apply to Christianity. The process of searching and the act of surrender can lead to other kinds of commitment, both religious and non-religious. What characterizes all of them is their shared *forms* of experience, irrespective of their *content*.

To recognize this is not the same as saying that all faiths are equal. From a biblical point of view, the content and object of faith make all the difference. To believe in astrology is not to believe in Christ by another name.

But from the standpoint of *how* we come to believe (in anything), the processes of faith development are not limited to developing faith in Christ. We see it in members of political parties who have given themselves wholly to the cause in which they believe; in sportsmen who have made their commitment to sport the centre of their lives; in those who have devoted their energies to community life and action. We see it, too, in members of other religions who, like the committed Christian, have moved beyond superficial adherence into heartfelt faith.

The owned faith of these individuals is every bit as real as full-hearted Christianity, though Christians would dispute the claim that the object of their faith was as worthy. The task of the evangelist is not to disparage such commitment but to preach Christ in such a way that his hearers may come to own a new faith in him.

CONCLUSION

We have looked in some detail at how children can be said to have faith, and have seen that it is possible to speak of faith in diverse, though connected, ways. Equally important, we have noted that a child's response of faith is not the same as that of an adult. Rather, he or she moves through stages of development, each of which (as we have seen) has its own characteristic response.

In all this, it needs to be stressed that whether we are talking about faith developmentally or theologically, we are still talking about faith as a gift from God. It is so because all God's creation must be regarded as gift. It is not something which just happens to 'be there': it is the deliberate handiwork of a loving Father.

When, therefore, we speak of children 'naturally' possessing faith, we are not speaking of something which has happened independent of God. He is the sustainer as well as creator of the natural processes, and a child's capacity to respond to the world around her and to persons (even God himself) is as much a gift as the lakes, mountains and valleys. A child's response to nature may, without her realizing it, be a response to the God who created nature and who has made us in his own image. We must never drive a wedge between creation and salvation: it is the same God who has brought about both; both are aspects of his loving purpose and it is God's Spirit who prompts the response of faith to both.

We can begin to see, then, that there are some questions which can only be answered theologically: What do we mean by speaking of creation and salvation as being tied together? How does Jesus Christ and his work of atonement fit into this? What do we mean by sin if children's behaviour is determined by the natural process of development? Does this rule out accountability before God? If parental love is so crucial to healthy development, how does the idea of God as Father fit in, particularly in a single-parent society? And what about conversion? Is there any room for it within stages of faith? Finally, what should we make of children and spiritual gifts, given the growing emphasis in some quarters upon the need to include them within the evangelistic message?

These are all large issues. In part two we shall consider them from a biblical and theological perspective. It will not be possible to arrive at final answers: theology is not like a Sherlock Holmes puzzle. We must remain open to the possibility that God will modify and even overturn our fallible human views. The best we can do is to submit both our questions and provisional answers to him and his word in the knowledge that he is faithful and will lead us into all truth.

NOTES TO CHAPTER 4

1. James Fowler, *Stages of Faith*, New York: Harper & Row 1981, p 151.
2. John Westerhoff III, *Will Our Children Have Faith?* New York: Seabury Press 1976, pp 94–96.
3. Westerhoff, as above, pp 91–103.

PART TWO

The theological framework

Developing a theology of children's ministry which relates to the theories of child development discussed in part one.

5
Why theology?

The relevance of theology to children's evangelism and ministry:

Attitudes to theology
Some reactions
The experience of the first Christians
Theological reflection today

What makes for effective evangelism? For many Christians the answer is simple: sharing our experience of Christ. But what does that involve? Again, for many the answer is straightforward: explaining to people what Jesus has done in our lives.

Now this is fine, as far as it goes. But it does not go far enough. As we have seen in part one, effective evangelism can be greatly enhanced by an understanding of theories of faith development. In the second half of this book we shall be looking at why theology is equally essential.

Attitudes to theology

We live, however, in an anti-theological age. In popular usage, 'theology' has become a synonym for something which is sterile and irrelevant. When someone says, 'Don't get too theological', what they mean is 'Don't start nitpicking!' Alternatively, theology is seen as another term for ideology which suggests rigidity and dogmatism. Either way, it is held in low esteem.

Unfortunately this attitude is held by a substantial number of Christians. While not always despised, theology is frequently downgraded or bypassed in favour of varieties of 'spiritual' experience. Why should this be so? There are, I think, four main reasons:

1. *We feel threatened by theology.* It is a fact that most of us strongly dislike jargon, whatever we are doing. The trouble with theology is that it so often seems to depend upon a great deal of jargon. Terms such as 'justification by faith', 'sanctification', 'atonement' (to mention but a few) abound. As a result, it becomes easier to avoid theological discussion altogether in favour of sharing experiences.

A related point lies in the fear of handling complex ideas and concepts. These are seen as the preserve of intellectuals. Since, on this line of reasoning, theology is full of ideas and concepts, it becomes much better to leave it to the intellectuals and get on with the task of practical Christian living.

2. *We distrust theologians.* There is a widespread feeling that whereas Christian faith is essentially simple and straightforward,

theologians have come along and made it complicated and unintelligible. Moreover, it is held that theologians (particularly of the more liberal kind) have more interest in undermining people's faith than in building it up. So, understandably, people steer clear of theology altogether.

3. *Theology as a discipline has become divorced from the pastoral life of the church.* The history of theology in Britain is that most modern research and thinking has been carried on in universities. In consequence, this has resulted in theology and pastoral practice splitting off from each other. One has remained the prerogative of the seminary, the other the preserve of the church. It is little wonder, therefore, that ordinary Christians have grown up without much theological knowledge on one hand, yet remain profoundly suspicious of it on the other.

4. *Pragmatism rules OK.* Pragmatism is the belief that the ultimate test of anything is not whether it is true but whether it works. According to this way of thinking, it is not principles which count but results. Now it takes only a little reflection to appreciate that this has come to dominate not just secular society but much of the thinking of Christians too. This is nowhere more true than in evangelism where the frequent assumption that big numbers automatically equal the activity of God needs to be seen for what it is – the product of unchristian pragmatism. The essential point in relation to theology is that, combined with a distrust of theologians, pragmatism has led many to emphasize activism as a substitute for theology.

For all these reasons, therefore, theology has fallen into disrepute with dangerous results both for the life of the church and for evangelism. (I should add here that by 'the church' I do not mean simply the institution but the whole body of Christian believers.)

Some reactions

One line of response to these developments would be to *deny that they matter*. 'So what if theology has been bypassed? God is not confined to concepts and ideas. Still less is he likely to work through unbelieving theologians. It is much more likely that he will reveal himself directly to individual Christians or groups who are open to his Spirit and who can share their experience of God with others.' This argument has the virtue of simplicity but it ignores the fact that all experiences have to be communicated and interpreted. Once we begin to do this, we engage in theology.

Perhaps this is the point at which to stress that at the heart of theology lies not a set of abstract ideas, but (as the term theology implies) the Word of God. The term *theology* is a compound of two Greek words meaning literally 'God' and 'Word'. Put this way, theology becomes less frightening. It ceases to be a matter of high-flown ideas and abstract concepts (though it can involve these) and becomes instead a matter of involvement with God as he reveals himself in his Son. It is no mere coincidence that in John's Gospel, Jesus is called the Logos – the Word – for it is in Christ that God has spoken. Jesus *is* God's Word.

It is important to understand, therefore, that when we describe theology as 'God words' we are not confining it to purely verbal or intellectual activity. The idea of the Word of God taken in its biblical context refers to the activity of God through his Son towards us as his creation.

A second response is *not to disown theology but to avoid it*. This usually takes the form of a statement such as, 'I'm not clever enough, I leave theology to those who are. My job is to get on with the practical side of things.' Such a view has to be examined very carefully; for it is almost certainly based upon the belief that theology is a matter for the intellect alone. Given this starting point the statement is logical enough. But a genuinely biblical approach sees theology as the relationship between the Word of God and the whole person. Once we realize this, we are freed from the tyranny of supposing theology to be the preserve of the highly educated. It can be experienced instead as the privilege of every Christian. In fact, whether we realize it or not, we all engage in theology from the moment we begin to reflect upon God. The key question is whether we are willing to think and act systematically about the Word of God. If not then our theology is likely to be a very hit-and-miss affair.

The third and most constructive response is to *enter into the theological task, seeing it as both a calling and gift for every Christian,* irrespective of age or intellectual ability. Of course, we are not all called to write learned treatises but we are each given the responsibility of understanding and sharing our faith with others. This is not first and foremost a question of sharing our *feelings* but of sharing the *content* of our belief. To illustrate this, we have to put ourselves back into the place of the first Christians.

The experience of the first Christians

In the New Testament we find three distinct groups of believers. The first were those who had known Jesus during his life and had experienced at first hand his death and resurrection. This group, therefore, had direct knowledge of Christ. The second group comprised those who had never known the Lord but who had heard about him and who had come to believe in him. The third group (if it can be called a group) included those to whom Christ had revealed himself directly after his ascension. Paul is the most obvious example of this.

Although all three groups had come to faith in different ways, they shared two elements in common. The first was that their belief was based on facts. They did not simply 'just believe' in some kind of mystical experience. Their belief arose out of the historical events concerning Jesus. They were not content to rely upon a feelings-based experience of the Spirit but were driven to fill out such experiences with facts about the life, death and resurrection of their Lord.

This brings us to the second element of their faith. As the first believers struggled to understand the meaning of what had happened to them, they found themselves having to draw upon theology. Their explanation of who Jesus was could not confine itself to purely historical statements about what he had done, where he had lived, how he had died and risen. It was simply too powerful to be limited to such categories. Instead, the Christians had to interpret all that had taken place by speaking in terms of God's power, his sending of his Son, his raising Jesus from death and the coming of the Spirit. Moreover, this theological explanation of events was held out as a challenge to all who listened. It was not a message solely for the already-believers, but was one which confronted would-be believers with the need to turn to the Jesus who had lived, died, risen and who now claimed their lives and loyalties.

So we see from the New Testament how the impact of the risen Christ forced the first believers into theology: there was no other way of expressing the meaning of their experience.

Theological reflection today

What I am suggesting is that although we may not have realized it, exactly the same kind of pattern can be found in the lives of Christians today. Even though we may not have thought that we were doing theology, we do it whenever we seek to understand and interpret our faith. The main difference between us and the first Christians is that none of us has ever known Jesus in the flesh and that consequently we draw upon the life, belief and experience of Christians through two thousand years to help us understand our own experience.

Theology, then, is essentially about reflecting upon our experience of God. Once we grasp this, there is no need for us to be overwhelmed or threatened by it. Like most things, it can be approached at different levels, some more difficult than others. But this does not mean it should never be approached at all – simply that we must find the appropriate level for ourselves and then get stuck in. After all, we do not avoid cooking just because we are not up to Cordon Bleu standard! If we did, we should all starve. The same is true of theology.

THE STRUCTURE OF PART TWO

In structuring the second part of this book I have, firstly, attempted to pick up some of the questions arising out of the study of development in part one. The issues of sin and account-ability, conversion, the family, and the parenthood of God are all relevant to the problems discussed earlier. At points, refer-ences are made back to Lee and Lizzie in order to demonstrate this.

Secondly, I have tried to group the discussion of these issues within a theological framework which is both biblical and coherent. Thus, we start with the creation and fall as the broad context in which to discuss the problem of sin and accountability, and then move to a consideration of atonement and redemption in order to ground our discussion of conversion. This is followed by a chapter looking at the theological basis of family and the appropriateness of the family image to describe the church. Finally, under the title 'what we teach', I have not so much set out a mini-systematic theology as discussed in some depth three major issues in modern children's ministry. These fit readily into a trinitarian framework: the idea of God as Father; the importance of God having come in the flesh through the incarnation; and (perhaps most controversial) the current debate about children and gifts of the Spirit. This final chapter, therefore, is very much geared to contemporary issues which have occasioned considerable discussion among children's workers. However, because I believe strongly in the importance of the Trinity as giving shape to our theology and experience, I have sought to organize these within a trinitarian structure.

There is much meat, then, in the chapters which follow. It is, nonetheless, meat which enables us to grow. It is my hope that the reader may enjoy a good meal!

6
Creation and Fall

Views of child development as they relate to doctrines of sin and accountability:

Whatever became of sin?
What is sin?
  Sin as a power
  Sin as a state
Theology versus social science?
  Man as a sinner: an integrationist approach
  Original sin: matching theology and development
Sin and accountability
  An age of accountability?
  Pointers from theology
  Insights from child development
  Conclusions drawn from the development models
A revised model for sin and accountability

As we saw with Lee and Lizzie, a child's awareness of the world around her develops over time. The same is true of her awareness of God. Theologically, we may say that she is created in God's image with an instinct for him – as Augustine put it, with a God-shaped gap which only God can fill.

How this develops will be affected by crucial factors outside the child's control. Her family, for example, may be opposed to Christian faith or, alternatively, simply not interested. Since the family is the most important context for nurture and growth, its attitude will be determinative for the child's faith development. Other important factors will be the attitude of teachers, friends and the media.

But in all this we have to recognize that children are not simply conditioned automatons devoid of their own wills. Though they will be conditioned to some extent, we must acknowledge both pragmatically and theologically that they retain some ability to choose, whether in the area of relationships, values or simple obedience and disobedience to rules. It is in this context that the problem of sin and accountability which has preoccupied children's evangelists for so long must be discussed.

Whatever became of sin?

In 1973 an American psychiatrist, Karl Menninger, published a book which rapidly became a best seller. Its title was *Whatever Became of Sin*? The reader of this present book may well feel the same. The models of child development we have looked at in part one could easily be taken to imply that the theological categories at the centre of Christian evangelism have been devalued or discarded. After all, if children go through processes of growth and development which are built into the created order, how can we say that the inevitable fruits of these processes should be counted as sinful? We might just as well say that big feet or fair hair are sinful. If so, what becomes of evangelism, let alone sin?

There are four possible approaches to this question. The first we might label *theological exclusivism*. If we follow this line, we dismiss models of development as irrelevant. What counts is theological explanation alone: 'We have practised evangelism for generations without the aid of Fowler, Westerhoff and the rest. There is no need to begin now, especially if they undermine Christian doctrine.'

The second we could call *psychological exclusivism*. This is the mirror image of the first approach. Human actions and experience are reduced to merely psychological explanations. Sin becomes a symptom and salvation a matter of therapy. Theology and religion can be totally explained away.

The third approach can be termed *compartmentalization*. This has the apparent advantage of embracing both theology and psychology equally. The difficulty is that it can only do so by confining them to separate compartments of life. Within their respective jurisdictions, each is authoritative but they do not interfere with each other. Thus theology governs the religious life, while psychology governs the mental life.

The fourth possibility is *integration*. This takes seriously the claims of both but seeks to relate them more adequately across the whole of life. Putting them in boxes is not enough.

Let's look at these four approaches through two examples.

In the first we must imagine that a child has stolen some sweets. He is from a poor home with unloving parents. His older brother has been convicted of theft. What are we to make of his action?

The theological exclusivist will say: 'He has sinned and that is that. He, like the rest of us, is a sinner by nature. He is guilty before God and man.'

The psychological exclusivist will say: 'He is the victim of his home circumstances and his inner drives. He could not help these. He cannot be blamed.'

The compartmentalist will say: 'Looked at theologically he has sinned. But looked at psychologically he has acted according to inner forces beyond his control. Both explanations have to be set alongside each other.'

The integrationist will go one step further. He will say: 'His inner drives correspond to the idea of sin as a power within us. His actions were wrong by any standard. He was responsible for his actions because he had a choice not to steal. But there are extenuating circumstances which must affect the way we look at the action, the limits of responsibility and the question of punishment.'

Now let's consider example number two.

Lee was defiant about taking his tricycle to the seaside. He went against the wishes of his parents. He argued and answered back. He threw a tantrum to force them to give in. How should we interpret Lee's actions?

The theological exclusivist will say that his behaviour is evidence of original sin. It is also probably actual sin because it is wilful disobedience of his parents, which is against God's law.

The psychological exclusivist will argue that Lee is simply establishing his sense of identity and that moral questions do not enter in.

The compartmentalist will note that these are two different ways of describing the same action, and depending upon what kind of account we want, we will opt for either a theological or psychological explanation.

And the integrationist will say that in establishing his identity, Lee has the potential either for self-centredness which is the root of all sin, or for a mature character able to make its own judgments. Much will depend upon whether he now begins to learn and accept that others too have wills and wishes which must be respected. Whatever happens, there will remain a residual core of self-will and self-centredness which might be called inbuilt sinfulness.

These examples suggest that evaluating sin and talking about it evangelistically are not always simple matters. This means that we must have a clear idea of what scripture means by sin and a clear understanding of the developmental processes of childhood. We shall then be in a position to consider the appropriate approach for evangelism.

What is sin?

Ask the legendary man or woman in the street what they understand by sin and you will almost certainly get a list of actions to avoid: the seven (or more) deadly sins. But this is misleading. In scripture, particularly in the writings of Paul, we find sin portrayed not so much as a series of specific offences as in terms of: (1) a power which controls us; and (2) a state in which we find ourselves.

Sin as a power

Both Jesus and Paul viewed sin as an occupying power which conquers and enslaves us. In John 8:34, Jesus declares, 'I tell you the truth, everyone who sins is a slave to sin.' Likewise, Paul declares that 'all men are . . . under the power of sin' (Rom 3:9, RSV) and speaks of Christians as once having been 'slaves to sin' (Rom 6:6). Addressed to believers in Rome, the image was doubly powerful for they knew exactly what slavery entailed.

Sin thus pictured can be compared to the slavemaster who cracks the whip over us at will. We are in bondage to him and cannot escape. Our lives are controlled by his harsh and cruel demands.

Our individual acts of sin are the evidence of his control. It is not that we are declared sinful because we commit sins. We sin because we are already controlled by the power of sin. The particular sins we engage in are simply the fruit of the principle of sin that is at work within us.

This is a crucial point of Christian doctrine. There are many people (some of them Christians) who believe that to be right with God is essentially a matter of ceasing to commit acts of sin. They are like the smoker who thinks that his problem will be solved by not buying cigarettes. But this is to miss the point. Sin, like smoking, is a question of addiction. It is not the individual items that have to be given up: it is the power or grip behind them which has to be dealt with.

An illustration from nature may help. Ask yourself what makes a cat a hunter. Is it the individual prey he catches, or does he catch the prey because he is by instinct already a hunter? The answer, of course, is that he hunts because it is part of his being. Bringing home a mouse or a bird does not make him a hunter: he hunts them because he is a hunter by nature. He would not be a cat otherwise.

This parallels our experience of sin. We sin because we are by nature sinners. We are not made sinners because we commit acts of sin. It is the occupying, controlling power of sin that makes us sinful and which must be destroyed.

Sin as a state

We are not only sinners by nature, we are sinners by choice. Sin therefore describes both the power that enslaves us and the state we find ourselves in before God. In Romans, Paul paints a picture of humanity having deliberately turned away from God. This chimes with Luther's description of us as being 'curved in upon ourselves'. We are oriented toward self and selfishness. This is what lies at the heart of idolatry:

> 'What may be known about God is plain to them [humanity], because God has made it plain to them. For since the creation of the world God's invisible qualities – his eternal power and divine nature – have been clearly seen, being understood from what has been made, so that men are without any excuse.
>
> For although they knew God, they neither glorified him as God nor gave thanks to him, but their thinking became futile and their foolish hearts were darkened . . . they exchanged the truth of God for a lie and worshipped and served created things rather than the Creator' (Rom 1:19–21, 25).

The logic of Paul's argument runs like this: through creation, we have known enough about God to acknowledge our dependence upon him and to realize that he has a claim upon us. But we (the human race) want to be independent of God. So we seek wisdom and security in creation and in human affairs. We live as if God did not matter. This has several disastrous results.

Firstly, we end up worshipping anything and everything other than God. By worship, Paul does not mean that we literally bow down before our cars, our possessions, our families and so on. He means that we give something other than God the central place in our lives. Whatever form this takes, it becomes an idol.

Secondly, the rejection of God leads to immorality. Again, Paul is not suggesting that everyone becomes a murderer or a thief. He is trying to show that society without God will find itself afflicted by all kinds of immorality because inborn sinfulness will rise up and take control.

Thirdly, once sin gains an entry it multiplies. Individually and socially, the human race becomes trapped in a downward spiral of ever increasing speed. Even if it wanted to free itself (which it doesn't), it could not.

It is at this point that voluntary sin is transformed into sin the slavemaster. What began as a deliberate choice now becomes an inescapable trap. The power of sin reigns.

All this means that our state of supposed independence is, in fact, the worst kind of bondage. For we are not only spiralling away from God and all that is good, but we do so in the illusion that it represents true freedom! It is little wonder that in 2 Corinthians, Paul refers to this as blindness (2 Cor 4:4).

A broken relationship

We need to note one further point. At bottom, sin is not a matter of breaking impersonal laws set up by an impersonal divine legislature. It is the breaking of a personal relationship with God. When we sin he is pained by the breach of friendship this entails. The Old Testament prophets saw this clearly. They characterize sin as the breaking of the covenant between Yahweh and his people. Israel's sin is tantamount to adultery – the breaking of the most intimate bond of all (Hos 2–3). The cry of the heartbroken husband echoes in God's word to Hosea: ' "She (Israel) decked herself with rings and jewellery, and went after her lovers, but me she forgot," declares the Lord.' (Hos 2:13). This – the deliberate breach of relationship – is what lies at the heart of sin.

Theology versus social science?

Whether we think of sin as a power or as a state, it is clear that the plight of humanity is desperate. We are gripped by the force of sin and held in a state which cuts us off from God and renders us worthy of condemnation. It amounts to a broken relationship that is not just the result of a falling out between man and God but a full-scale rebellion. The end result will be either reconciliation or rejection.

How should we match this with the findings of child development and, when we have done so, what are the implications for evangelism?

We are faced with two sets of facts. One is theological: it tells us about the human condition viewed from a biblical perspective. Its primary concern is to set out the relationship of man to God, though in doing so, it also speaks of the disrupted nature of relationships within the human race. The second is drawn from the social sciences. Its concern is to explain what we know (or think we know) about the observable processes of human development. It is not necessarily anti-theological but it has been used in this way. For this reason, many Christians are profoundly and understandably suspicious.

This has been unfortunate. It has led to evangelism and Christian nurture being uninformed by the study of how children develop. And in reverse, it has led to the assumption on the part of some developmentalists that the Christian faith has nothing to say of any value.

These two forms of exclusivism have impoverished ministry to children. It is conceivable that they have done real damage to children's spiritual growth. In refusing to take account of each other, they have either ignored vital spiritual truths or they have disparaged the new knowledge we have steadily gained about how children grow up. There is much to be repented of on both sides: the evangelist who says that he has nothing to learn from the developmentalist is no less guilty than the developmentalist who declares the Christian faith to be irrelevant. Openness and humility are needed on both sides.

The compartmentalist model tries to take account of this but it offers little practical way forward. Its strength is that it recognizes the importance of both theology and child development. But its weakness is that it fails to show how they are related. It can only say that each is a truthful account in its own way and invite us to choose whichever we want.

The integrationist view, however, is not satisfied with such an approach. It seeks to find a means of applying both theological and developmental insights without putting them into separate boxes. How does this work out in practice?

Man as a sinner: an integrationist approach

Let us take *the idea of man as a sinner*. If we compare the teaching of Paul with the arguments of modern psychologists, we seem to have two contradictory and incompatible positions. Whereas Paul speaks of man choosing sin, a psychologist may well speak of the irresistible and uncontrollable forces within us which determine our behaviour. Whereas Paul may describe man as having deliberately rejected God in favour of self-reliance, the psychologist may claim that the notions of independence and self-confidence are essential to healthy personality. Whereas Paul condemns self-centredness, the psychologist may reply that from birth we are necessarily conditioned to look after number one. If we did not do so we would not survive. And so on.

The integrationist approach therefore seems doomed from the start. It would appear that we are not just describing the same thing differently, but that we are faced with two incompatible accounts of what sin actually is.

But is this necessarily true? The first point to note is that although Paul describes the effects of sin, he nowhere gives a detailed explanation of the processes involved beyond the combination of theology and common sense contained in Romans 6 and 7. Even there he is concerned primarily with the spiritual and theological dimensions.

What is equally striking, however, is that neither in his review of how the human race came to choose sin (Rom 1) nor in his discussion of how sin entered through Adam (Rom 5), does Paul attempt to explain exactly the means by which these happened. He is content to state in a broad way that we have deliberately chosen sin rather than God and that Adam's sin represents man's first such choice, but Paul does not venture beyond that. His primary goal is to enable his readers to make *theological* sense of their *personal experience* of sin and to understand that in Christ there is freedom and reconciliation. Although he shows deep psychological insight, Paul is not interested in being an early developmental psychologist.

If we accept this, we are freed to look again at the developmental evidence. We can begin by asking what the explanations of child development and behaviour are trying to do. The answer is that they are trying to give an account of how we grow up and the kind of common patterns that are observable in children's experience. *In themselves*, these accounts do not rule out God's involvement: if such an assumption is made, it is the result of a *prior* decision to exclude theology, or to relegate the activity of God to a supernatural plane, strictly apart from the natural.

In giving an account or accounts of human growth, the social scientist is simply putting observable characteristics into some kind of pattern and trying to suggest how they have come to be.

An example

Let's go back to the child who stole sweets. The questions to ask are: (1) Did he know stealing was wrong? If he did not, then he can hardly be put in the same category as a child who knows what theft is and still goes ahead with it. If he did, however, we must suppose that, assuming he was not forced to steal by a parent, brother or bully, he could have chosen not to and therefore must be held accountable for his actions. (2) What led him to steal? Was it greed, poverty, trying to impress his friends, or what? Here the psychologist can be of great help. He may point to the child's poor home, or the fact that everyone in his home steals and so the child has simply acquired what he wants in the way all his family do. Nevertheless, if he knew theft was wrong and chose it still, he is accountable.

We can hold theft to be a sin, therefore, but still recognize the role of psychological factors in leading a person to sin. The fact that it is possible to supply a non-theological account of how the sin arose does not invalidate the theological significance of the action: theft is sin nonetheless, but extenuating circumstances may modify our attitude to questions of responsibility and punishment. The child may be warned rather than prosecuted.

Original sin: matching theology and development

Another way of looking at integration is to try to match the theological and developmental accounts feature by feature. This may not be possible at all points but there are some where it is. To demonstrate, we shall focus on *the idea of original sin*.

Although Paul nowhere uses the term 'original sin', the notion of inborn sinfulness is prominent in his thinking. Indeed, that is the idea behind Paul's discussion of Adam and Christ in Romans 5: we all share in Adam's sinfulness and are therefore slaves to sin. When we look at what inborn sinfulness is we find that the ideas of theology and psychology come very close to each other, although they do not use the same language.

The reality
At the core of Paul's definition of sin lies the notion of self-centredness: Luther's idea of being curved in upon oneself. It is not just that we care about ourselves but that we are concerned for ourselves above all else. When the chips are down, it is number one that counts. Even when the chips are *not* down, we seek to gain the most for ourselves out of any situation, even at the expense of others.

The developmentalist will say that such behaviour is characteristic of all young children. As we noticed in the cases of Lee and Lizzie, the first months and years of life are built upon the perception that the world revolves around supplying the infant's needs. In this sense there is an inborn self-centredness in us all. It is part of what it means to be human.

But that is exactly Paul's point: to be human is to be born sinful because to be born human means to be born self-centred. Paul and modern psychology both agree that self-centredness is a trait we are all born with. So the developmentalist's observable evidence of inborn self-centredness corresponds to Paul's theological idea of inborn sinfulness.

Choice
At what point does inborn sinfulness or self-centredness become deliberate sin? Here again, we find a match between theology and psychology. In addition to viewing sin as a power and a state, Paul characterizes sinfulness in two further ways. On one hand it is a rejection of God and, on the other, a lack of love for other people. The psychologist may have nothing to say about the first, but it is the view of all psychological theories that healthy personal development is achieved only by learning to respect others. Put another way, the mature individual is one who relates to other people not because of what they can *supply* but because of what they *are* – valuable persons in their own right. And the healthiest community is one in which people do things for one another out of generosity.

The self-centredness of natural growth first becomes wilful sin, then, when we deliberately choose to elevate our own desires above those of others. This involves, of course, the capacity to recognize the existence of other people's rights. As we shall see in our later discussion of accountability, such a capacity does not develop *fully* until teenage years, but once it becomes possible to say, 'That person has equal rights to mine but I shall do my utmost to make sure that I always come off best', the threshold of wilful sin has been crossed. We have all met children as well as adults who are simply 'users' of others. Even when they appear to care for somebody else, it is still essentially a route to personal advancement. Such people are exaggerated forms of what we all are: sinners curved in upon ourselves.

The relationship of theology and child development, therefore, can be shown to be complementary provided the limitations and claims of each are understood. There will be occasions when it becomes difficult to see how they match. But the proper response at that point should be not to reject one in favour of the other or to say that one is superior to the other, but either to accept that their relationship is not clear and live with the gap between them or to keep on working at a resolution. Given that both have valuable insights into the human condition, it would be irresponsible to write off one simply because at first glance there seem to be elements that cannot be reconciled.

Sin and accountability

The question of what we should make of sin leads us into another crucial area. Whenever children's workers get together to discuss theology, one question above all comes to dominate the discussion: the spiritual status of the child. This is hardly surprising since a children's worker will find that the position he takes on this issue will determine the goal of his ministry. In this section we shall be assessing the main views in the debate, from the standpoint of accountability and responsibility. We shall be asking how far these concepts are applicable to children and, if so, what follows in terms of communicating the gospel.

The alternative theological positions essentially boil down to:

1. Because of original sin, all children are condemned until they positively trust in Christ.

2. Children of believing parents are covered by their parents' faith and are included within the atonement until they refuse Christ.

3. Despite original sin, children of unbelieving parents are covered by the atonement since God is both loving and just.

Although recent writers have been hesitant to endorse position 1 outright, it was staunchly advocated by R Hudson Pope, one of the main figures in the history of Scripture Union. In his book *To Teach Others Also*, Pope was unequivocal in expounding the view that all children, unless they had made an open profession of faith, should be regarded as lost. It is worth quoting his argument at length since it is a trenchant statement of the school of thought he represented and which was dominant in children's evangelism for many years:

> 'What then is the state of the child? It is either (a) A born-again child, truly converted to God, a child of God by faith in Christ Jesus, a child of light; or (b) An unconverted child of Adam, wrong in heart, and, according to age and opportunity, wrong also in practice. . . It is hard to accept statements about children 'going astray' and 'perishing', for most of them seem such jolly little people. . . The fact is that, until the grace of God does its wonderful work, the child has a sinful heart and will pursue a sinful course.'[1]

Pope's view, then, is crystal clear: children are condemned until positively and evidently born again.

> 'We look at the outward appearance and in some children we see little evidence of sinfulness. But let us not be deceived; "God looketh on the heart", and if we want to know what the heart of an unsaved child is like, we shall find the answer in our Lord's own words in St Mark 7:21 – "For from within, out of the heart of men proceed evil thoughts, adulteries, fornications, murders, thefts, covetousness, wickedness, deceit, lasciviousness, an evil eye, blasphemy, pride, foolishness." This is our Lord's picture of the human heart, even the

heart of a child, for he makes no age limit.'[2]

Two observations are pertinent. Firstly, Pope makes no distinction between inborn sinfulness and conscious sin – it is all equally damnable in God's sight; and, secondly, Pope's view makes no allowance for age. It does not matter whether your sin is unwitting or deliberate, or whether you are nine months or ninety: you are equally accountable before God. This, as we shall see, requires careful and critical examination if we are to do justice to biblical theology and to what we have learned about child development.

At the other end of the spectrum from Hudson Pope lies John Inchley, author and Scripture Union evangelist. In his view, *all* children, whether from Christian homes or not, are included within the atoning work of Christ until they reject him. On one level, it seems that this argument rests on an unspoken *emotional* premise: how could a loving God condemn innocent children? But on a more rational level, it is grounded in theology. For central to Inchley's view is the belief that children belong to God from birth. This he deduces from the Gospel passages which show Jesus accepting children:

> 'In chapters 18 and 19 of Matthew's Gospel, and the corresponding passages in Mark 10 and Luke 18, we have recorded the words and acts of Jesus himself which encourage us to believe that all children are both important and acceptable to our heavenly Father. . . Jesus spoke of the kingdom belonging to them. In their case, however, this was not for any reason of race or of possible Christian parent relationship, and certainly not because of childlike worthiness or coming to Jesus in repentance and faith in an adult-orientated way. It was only through God's grace and because of the atoning work of Christ.'[3]

The conclusion he draws is no less forthright than that of Hudson Pope, albeit completely opposite:

> 'We believe that all children are included in the great atoning sacrifice and belong to Jesus Christ until they deliberately refuse him.'[4]

It is important to grasp that John Inchley believes in inborn sinfulness as much as does Hudson Pope. Moreover, he is firm in his conviction that new birth is a necessity. The point of difference arises from Inchley's view that God's judgment is directed against those who deliberately and knowingly reject the gospel rather than those (such as children) who cannot be held accountable for ignorance or immaturity. Consequently,

> 'In God's good time it is expected that they [children] will acknowledge the rule and reign of God and possess the kingdom for themselves by the illumination and calling of the Holy Spirit and by the birth which is from above.'[5]

The crux of the argument, then, lies in the notion of accountability. In what way (if any) do we believe that God holds children responsible for their sinfulness or their deeds?

An age of accountability?

The problem of child accountability has been recognized for a long time. The traditional answer has been given in terms of an *age of accountability*. Ron Buckland defines this as 'usually understood in negative terms, ie as a time when the child, if he rejects Christ, is open to the just judgment of God.'[6]

The notion of a fixed and specific *point* of accountability, however, has come under fire. John Inchley has summed up the feelings of many when he comments that, 'Any attempt to pinpoint a moment in the life of a child as being the actual age of accountability will be met with disappointment.'[7] Inchley is happier to speak of a 'time of accountability' rather than a static point. The reasons for this unease are not hard to find.

First, commonsense observation, as well as scientific study, suggests that *children undergo development in their ability to discern right and wrong* and in their capacity to make moral-cum-spiritual decisions. This would suggest, in turn, that the notion of a fixed point at which a child becomes responsible must be abandoned. Instead we must begin to think of a series of points over time at which a child becomes increasingly responsible and therefore increasingly accountable.

Secondly, although there are common patterns in child development, *children are amazingly varied in the speeds at which they develop*. If this is true, it becomes impossible to fix upon a single age common to *all* youngsters at which they become accountable. The age at which they do become so will vary with each child and will take account of a complex of factors – mental, emotional, moral and spiritual, cultural and physical, the effects of nurture, experience and conditioning.

Thirdly, we can be helped in our thinking by *noticing what the law of the land makes of accountability*. In many ways, the question is similar both for the Christian trying to assess how far a child is accountable to God for acts of wrongdoing, and the legislator trying to draw up rules for determining when a child must be held accountable to human laws. It is significant that the law recognizes rising degrees of responsibility for criminal actions between the ages of ten and seventeen. Only when a person reaches seventeen is he treated as an adult. Moreover, justice by common consent requires flexibility in punishment according to circumstances. Even though two children may commit identical crimes, their differences of background, motive and intention, have to be taken into account. In the end a magistrate may decide that one should be held more accountable than the other because he is able to exercise a greater degree of responsibility. So it is clear that the matter of accountability is a complex one and that the notion of a single fixed point applicable to all children in all circumstances at all times is an illusion.

If we apply these reflections to the theological realm, it would seem that we cannot hold to a simple idea of an age of accountability. Are we therefore reduced to saying that children should not be regarded as responsible at all?

It would be easy either to take this line uncritically or to advocate the opposite: that children are just as accountable as adults. I would argue, however, that both of these alternatives are unsatisfactory and that the third way, the concept of developing accountability, will enable us to take both sin and accountability seriously.

Pointers from theology
It is important to recognize one crucial theological fact: nowhere in scripture do we find the biblical writers concerned with the questions which agitate us so greatly. They simply did not think

in our categories. It was not an issue for them whether children were to be regarded as saved or lost: the question never occurred to them. We will search in vain for a discussion of the destiny of non-adults.

If nothing else, this should make us wary of dogmatic conclusions. Given that scripture contains no direct discussion of the problem (indeed, it does not see any problem), it follows that any conclusions we may arrive at will be inferences from wider doctrines of man, salvation and God. When cases have been argued and positions staked out, it needs to be remembered that a large dose of humility is still required. If we are to be *true to* scripture we cannot legitimately infer that which is not *warranted by* scripture.

Paul's discussion of sin in Romans 1–5, for example (whether understood as a power or a state), says nothing about children. As we have seen, it is taken up with the status of the human race as a whole and even here the thought is of the adult race. As he declares that no one can claim to be righteous before God (Rom 3:23), Paul has nowhere in mind the question of children. The examples he uses to illustrate our wilful rebellion are all adult-centred: idolatry, sexual degradation, lust, murder, slander (1:18–31). 'God gave them over to a depraved mind' (1:26). Now it is impossible to read into this a simple doctrine of child sin unless we are prepared, against the evidence of the text, to say that Paul *was* thinking of children as he wrote. But that is plainly beyond the scope of the passage. Can we really believe that Paul is accusing children of sexual depravity, lust, murder and the rest? No, the most that we can say about the meaning of the text is that Paul was writing to make it clear that no one can claim righteousness on the basis of obedience to the law or any human standard. Such claims, of course, were adult in character.

To say this is not to deny the reality of inborn sinfulness. We are all offspring of Adam and this produces in us a desire for independence and self will which is the essence of sin. But again, we have to recognize that nowhere does Paul develop this thought in the context of children. His discussion in Romans 5 is designed to contrast the plight of man by nature with the salvation wrought by Christ. Although his argument assumes the reality of inborn sinfulness, if we are to be true to the text we have to acknowledge that Paul does not address the question of children, and that his concern is to show his (adult) readers the depth of what God has done in Christ.

We are left, then, with a major problem. The key biblical passages which address the questions of sin and salvation do not seem to be designed to answer our particular set of child-centred questions. Does this mean that the questions are invalid or unanswerable? Must we simply accept that we can say nothing about how the great Christian doctrines apply to children?

Fortunately not. The Bible does contain some clues but they are nowhere as clear or systematic as some writers have suggested or as we might wish.

Christian households

The first clue lies in Paul's admonitions to Christian households. In Colossians 3:20 he exhorts children to obey their parents 'for this pleases the Lord.' The implication is that disobedience will displease the Lord and thereby constitute sin. Similarly, in Ephesians children are commanded to obey their parents 'in the Lord' because this is right and because it will bring blessing from God. Not to do so would be a transgression. To underline the point, Paul cites the commandment, 'Honour your father and mother'.

It is clear from these passages that *children could and did sin*. The principle of inborn sinfulness did not simply come into play at adulthood. But beyond the *fact* of child sinfulness neither Paul nor the other New Testament writers were prepared to go.

Jesus and the children

The second clue lies in Jesus' attitude to children. There are a number of passages in the Gospels which feature Jesus and children. But as Hans-Ruedi Weber has pointed out,[8] these are not always straightforward and we must beware of reading back into the texts our own meanings. However, examination of Mark 9:36–37 reveals three aspects of Jesus' attitude to children:

'And he took a child and put him in the midst of them; and taking him in his arms, he said to them, "Whoever receives one such child in my name receives me; and whoever receives me, receives not me but him who sent me." '

First, we see that *Jesus commends children to our loving care*. In the New Testament the expression 'to receive somebody' always indicates warm and open hospitality. Moreover, in the Jewish environment, this idea included adoption of orphans into the family as if they were one of the family's own. By literally opening his arms to a child, therefore, Jesus was demonstrating the kind of love God expects us to show towards children.

Second, *Jesus points to a special relationship*. 'Whoever receives one such child in my name. . .' Behind this formula lies a very powerful idea. In Semitic thought, a king would send his representative to act on his behalf bearing the formula 'in my name'. The representative was to be seen as having as much importance as the king himself. As one rabbi put it, 'the envoy of the king is as the king himself'. Jesus, in effect, is declaring a child to be the envoy of God!

Such a thought must have seemed shocking to the disciples. We know from the next chapter that they tried to send the children away (Mark 10:13–16). But Jesus affirmed his (and therefore his Father's) special relationship with them by forbidding the disciples to dismiss them, and by blessing them.

Third, *the presence of the children signified the presence of the kingdom* (Mark 10:16). This is an extension of the previous idea. If the children are representatives of God, then God's kingdom must be present. Jesus does not explain in detail how this is so but Weber sums it up thus:

'It is the relationship with Jesus which makes these children representatives of God. As such they are our teachers. In their objective humility and need, they cry "mother", "father", "Abba", and they stretch out their empty hands. If we want to learn how to become God's representatives, we must learn it from the child in our midst.'[9]

The attitude of Jesus to children, therefore, unlike the general attitude of his day, was to welcome and accept children as loved by God and as metaphors of God's presence. This gives positive and biblical reinforcement to our belief that the atoning love of God covers children.

Insights from child development

It will already be apparent that I believe the best way of understanding accountability is in terms of development. There is no single point at which children universally, or individually, suddenly become accountable: each moves through an increasing degree of accountability until he or she reaches full responsibility in adulthood. This seems to fit most readily with what we have noted about the biblical categories of sin and salvation.

The strength of this approach is that it takes seriously the models of development we have already examined in part one. In pre-modern times, children were regarded from many points of view as mini-adults. Family organization in pre-industrial England assumed that as soon as they could fulfil basic physical tasks, children should play their part in the economy of the household. So it was that they worked in the fields, and later, in the factories of the industrial revolution. They were expected to behave like adults. Examples of this today can be seen in some African societies where the western ethos has not taken hold.

Children in western societies, however, are separated from the adult world at a very early age by school and pre-school institutions designed to reinforce childhood as a distinct phase of development in its own right. We do not recognize that adulthood has been attained until they reach eighteen. The fact that until recently the dividing line was drawn at twenty-one shows how relative the notion of an age of accountability is.

In order to develop a framework of spiritual accountability, therefore, we need to find a model or combination of models of child development which will address the kind of questions we face when asking what it means to be responsible before God. These can be found by comparing the faith models offered by Fowler and Westerhoff with research carried out in the field of *personal moral development*. Here questions about the development of children's attitudes to right and wrong parallel theological questions about their understanding of sin.

Many contemporary researchers in child development, inspired by the work of Piaget and Kohlberg, indicate the processes of change which take place in children as their cognitive capacities and moral awareness develop. Though not all would now follow them in detail, the proposed stages of Piaget and Kohlberg still indicate the directions of much research. We do not have to accept them uncritically to appreciate that there is much to learn from the basic tenets of their work.[10] The models we shall look at below should not therefore be taken as 'gospel' but as working theories to help us understand more about child development. Like all models, they remain open to debate and modification.

Piaget's model of moral development

On the basis of several carefully constructed experiments with groups of children, Piaget concluded that moral development moves through four stages. The first or *motor* stage coincides with early infancy up to two years old. During this period, behaviour is governed by what a child can do physically. The essential goal of a child is to fulfil certain basic tasks, and ideas of right and wrong are strictly related to the fulfilment of those tasks. Thus 'going to the potty' becomes right and making a mess on the floor wrong. Likewise, when a small child learns to walk we show our approval by telling her what a good girl she is. Morality for the child at this stage is a matter of successfully completing these physical tasks.

Stage two is known as the *egocentric* stage, and lasts from two to five years old. Although a child may learn simple rules for social behaviour, she is still fundamentally self-centred. She believes the world is constructed to meet her needs (a hangover from the baby and infant stages) and is not too bothered about others except insofar as they meet her needs. Her definition of right and wrong is what she can get away with in order to satisfy her desires.

In stage three (six to ten years), the child begins to develop an awareness of *social cooperation*. She will play with other children and there is some understanding of the need to obey rules. But even in games (at least in the first half of this phase), the child still continues to act individualistically. The notion of right and wrong as cooperation within a team is still vague.

The fourth and final stage Piaget identifies as beginning at eleven. In this, children become increasingly aware of *moral responsibility* towards other persons and therefore start to fix rules in detail, acknowledging that these must be universally and fairly applied. Right and wrong become related to abstract values and standards and the abstract idea of justice takes hold. Prior to this, morality has been a matter of concrete situations. A change in notions of morality and responsibility is beginning to take place.

Piaget lays considerable stress upon the place of rules in children's morality. This is important since it corresponds to the Christian view of the role of law in defining sin. Clearly, insight into how children develop their understanding of rules will help us in our search for a concept of accountability.

Piaget discovered three phases in children's attitudes to rules:

1. The first phase coincides with the motor stage outlined above and the first part of the egocentric stage. The infant begins with no conception of rules but by the end has some inkling of their importance. However, they are seen as examples rather than generally binding obligations. Thus a child may be told that sharing sweets is a good thing and may copy an act of sharing. But he may not make the jump to seeing this as a good thing in all circumstances and indeed is likely to hoard rather than share. The abstract notions of fairness and generosity are beyond his ability to comprehend.

2. Next comes what Piaget calls the transcendental phase. This lasts from about four years old to about eight. Children are aware of rules but see them as sacred and untouchable. They come from adults and can't be changed or questioned.

3. The third phase moves the child into the realm of moral consent. Rules are necessary to govern social relations and to ensure fair play but they can be altered by agreement. The underlying attitude is one of mutual respect for the rights of others. There is a keen awareness of fairness as an overarching value. Justice becomes crucial, and if rules do not promote justice they can be bent or disregarded without such action being seen as immoral.

We can see from Piaget's scheme that the adult notions of sin and responsibility presumed in Paul's discussion of accountability in Romans can hardly apply to children whose notion even of what a rule is does not develop until junior school age. Moreover, to hold children accountable for failing to live up to abstract rules of right and wrong when they have not developed the capacity to appreciate abstractions (ie before eleven) hardly fits with biblical teaching about the just character of God.

Kohlberg and moral development

Building on the work of Piaget, Lawrence Kohlberg has developed a more sophisticated model based on six stages, grouped in three sets of two:

A. The pre-moral level

Stage 1: The child defines right and wrong by whether an action brings punishment. Rightness is not a matter of doing right according to some underlying moral order but simply avoiding punishment.

Stage 2: The right thing to do is what brings reward. Other people are not valuable in themselves but as instruments for getting what we want.

B. The conventional level

Stage 3: The child conforms to standards of right and wrong for fear of disapproval by others, especially adults. Kohlberg calls this the 'Good Boy-Nice Girl' stage. (Many adults' attitudes toward God are stuck at this level.)

Stage 4: Right is defined by obedience to authority. Rules are to be obeyed because they are right in themselves, irrespective of their content. So if a teacher concocts a game which has an element of injustice in it, it is always right to obey the teacher even though this may involve injustice.

C. The principled level

Stage 5: Morality is a matter of sticking to generally agreed rules. These are seen as necessary to protect individual rights. They can be changed by social agreement but individuals are not free to break them at will. Thus the rules of a game may be changed provided everyone agrees but one player alone may not act outside the rules for his own benefit.

Stage 6: Right and wrong are defined by a person freely choosing standards and principles for himself. Morality is not a matter of living up to others' expectations but of making up one's own mind. Personal rules should, however, respect the just rights of others and not be merely self-serving.

If we accept the basic direction of Piaget's and Kohlberg's work, it seems clear that the growth of adult moral capacity is a lengthy and complex process. Although since his original work Kohlberg has modified his model to recognize that few people ever reach the fullness of stage six, adult moral responsibility is nevertheless reckoned in terms of:

1. awareness of the rights of others;
2. ability to accept obligations arising from abstract values;
3. willingness to forgo self-centredness;
4. making up one's own mind.

Conclusions drawn from the development models

How do these models help us in our theological understanding of accountability?

The first and most important insight they offer is to provide *confirmation that responsibility and therefore accountability should be seen in terms of development*. The degree to which children should be held responsible for their actions must reflect the stage they have reached along the developmental line.

In practical terms, this will mean that we will not seek to hold children accountable for a stage of moral capacity they have not yet reached. A junior child, for example, can be held responsible for his attitude to concrete rules which govern specific kinds of situations but it is no good expecting him to reason in terms of abstract values. We could rightly expect obedience, for example, to the rule 'do not steal from shops', or 'do not hit your sister to get her sweets'. These are both specific and concrete. But we could not fairly expect a child to translate into practice such abstract principles as, 'honesty is a good thing' or 'violence and covetousness are wrong'. Accountability for failing to live up to abstractions must await adolescence. It is perhaps no coincidence that the biblical command to obey one's parents is a very concrete moral instruction.

Secondly, it follows that *it would be unjust to condemn a child for not living up to a law of God designed to be fulfilled by adults*. We cannot expect children in Kohlberg's stages one and two to live as if they were in stages five or six. To do so is unjust and unrealistic. It is the moral equivalent of expecting an infant who had just learned to count to solve differential equations.

These insights will affect the way we approach the themes of sin and atonement. If we are wise we will not assume that adult-oriented categories can be applied in a straightforward way to children. When we speak of them as sinners, we shall be careful to think of sin in appropriate terms. With respect to Hudson Pope, we shall not make the mistake of confusing biblical texts directed at adults with the spiritual status of children. We shall certainly not assume that the heart of a child is simply the heart of an adult in a smaller body.

On the other hand, we shall not avoid the question of accountability by assuming that children are free from sin altogether. That is not the proper inference to be drawn either from Paul or from the study of development. The issue is not whether children are accountable or not, but *what kind* of accountability is appropriate. As I have tried to show, we should hold a child responsible only at the level which he has reached. To do otherwise would be to deny both God's justice and his love.

A revised model for sin and accountability

If we bring together all the models of development we have so far discussed, one fact is clear: that sin means something radically different to a child of three from what it means to a child of fifteen. It is not just that some sins seem childish and others adult; the two children have vastly different capacities to comprehend the idea of sin. This seems common sense but, as we have seen from the arguments advanced by Hudson Pope, evangelists have not always recognized it either theologically or practically.

Once we accept that the meaning of sin varies from one stage of development to another, it follows that the meaning of accountability must vary likewise.

In the infant stage, a child operates entirely at the instinctive, discovery level. The ingredients of moral or spiritual understanding are undeveloped. Both sin and accountability are inappropriate categories.

In the late infant/early junior stage, the young child is learning to test limits even further. He knows what it means to say 'no' and to disobey. Wilful identity is starting to develop but right and wrong are still defined by what parents say. If 'sin' has any meaning at all it is in terms of disobeying parents. But even here the intellectual dimension of sin is missing. The decision to disobey is not based on a knowledge of what right and wrong are, or on being able to work out what they mean in practice. It is not a rational decision at all.

In the junior stage, the growing child defines right and wrong in terms of obeying (a) his group of friends and their code; and (b) rules and commands imposed by adults. His understanding of sin is more complex but he conceives of it in concrete terms. He must still be held responsible for acts of disobedience but his understanding is limited by his mental apparatus which is geared to concrete ways of thinking.

Theologically, therefore, sin for the child means definite, specific, concrete actions. Abstract concepts such as lovelessness or injustice are meaningless without concrete examples within the scope of the child's experience. To tell a child that sin is breaking God's law will not mean much. Telling him that sin is stealing someone's sweets or bashing his enemy in the playground will carry the message home.

At this stage, also, the idea of sin as an offence against God as a person who is distinct from parents begins to take shape. Although right and wrong have been associated primarily with commands issued by tangible, visible human adults, children in junior years increasingly become aware of God as a being distinct from Mum or Dad, who lays down a code of right and wrong which even adults must obey!

In the adolescent stage, the child's increasing ability to handle abstract concepts and to move from concrete, specific instances of wrongdoing to general rules about right and wrong means that he is close to being able to understand fully biblical teaching on sin. There is a growing awareness of sin as something which brings pain to God because it undermines the basis of covenant love. Sin thus becomes not simply a matter of breaking rules but of destroying a relationship. Although junior children may be able to glimpse something of this, it is only the flowering during adolescence of the ability to take another person's perspective (empathy) that allows a child to grasp the full meaning of sin – that it is a heartbreaking experience for God which can be dealt with only by the heartbreaking suffering love of the Son of God.

During this stage, therefore, it becomes possible to speak of sin both as a breaking of universal divine laws and as a disruption of the relationship of love between God and man. Since the child's understanding of justice is also developing at this time, the idea of sin as an injustice towards God may carry real meaning.

Where does this leave us in relation to accountability and the argument between Hudson Pope and John Inchley? In my view, the balance of the argument lies with Inchley. Given what we know about stages of faith and child development, it is both unjust and unrealistic to think that children below adolescence should be held responsible for sin viewed from an adult perspective. Moreover, our theology of God and God's character means that while we must recognize he does not take sin lightly (hence the atonement), his love and justice rule out the idea of holding a person accountable for that which he can neither understand nor fulfil.

This is not to say that sin does not matter or that it is not real prior to adolescence. Far from it. But its meaning is significantly different. A baby in the shopping trolley who takes sweets from the shelf at the supermarket and then eats them on the spot may be doing something undesirable (at least from the mother's point of view). But the twelve year old who deliberately does the same thing with the intention of avoiding payment is in a different category altogether. We would not dream of judging the two identically; and so it is with sin and accountability. When we reach the stage of intentionally, wilfully and repeatedly refusing God, then we have entered into the fullness of sin and God will reckon us wholly accountable. The atonement may cover those who do not fully understand what it means to break God's heart or do not know they are doing it, but for those who know and delight in sin, there must either be repentance, forgiveness and renewal or, ultimately, condemnation. But until such time as a child is able to understand and consciously *reject* Christ, we must assume that the love, mercy and justice of God are met in the atoning work of his suffering servant Son. If the gospel means anything it surely means this.

CONCLUSION

The argument of the last chapter can be summed up as follows:

1. There is no necessary conflict between developmental and

theological accounts of human sinfulness. They can be integrated at a number of crucial points.

2. Both psychology and scripture affirm the reality and power of self-centredness which lies at the heart of sin.

3. A child's understanding of the meaning of sin is relative to the stage of moral, emotional, educational and spiritual development he has reached.

4. The notion of accountability must likewise relate to stages of growth. It is better to speak of a continuum of accountability rather than a moment or age of accountability.

5. It is unjust to impose on children definitions of sin and accountability which presuppose adult capacities.

6. God's love, mercy and justice require that we do not speculate about the judgment of God further than scripture allows. Given all the considerations above, this means we shall include children within the atonement.

NOTES TO CHAPTER 6

1. R Hudson Pope, *To Teach Others Also*, London: CSSM, 1959, p 15.
2. Pope, as above, p 15.
3. John Inchley, *All About Children*, Eastbourne: Coverdale, 1976, p 31.
4. Inchley, as above, p 25.
5. Inchley, as above, p 37.
6. Ron Buckland, *Children and the King*, Surrey Hills: Anzea, 1979, p 68.
7. Inchley, as above, p 130.
8. Hans-Reudi Weber, *Jesus and the Children*, Geneva: WCC 1979.
9. Weber, as above, p 51.
10. Margaret Donaldson in *Children's Minds* (Fontana, 1978) has taken issue with Piaget and Kohlberg. She maintains that a child's perception of right and wrong has less to do with age than with the context in which he or she is introduced to notions of right and wrong. On this argument even a young child can understand basic rules and the need to obey them. This is a useful insight to have alongside Piaget and Kohlberg and reminds us that their framework must not be taken inflexibly. Nevertheless, I remain convinced that the sequence outlined by Piaget must continue to form the basis of our understanding of child development, *provided that* the importance of nurture (as indicated by Donaldson) is taken into account.

7
Atonement and Redemption

The interdependence of faith development and conversion; relating this to evangelism and nurture:

The faith status of children
  Traditional evangelical assumptions
What is conversion?
  John Westerhoff: Faith stages
  James Fowler: Faith content and conversion
Integration
The New Testament and conversion
  'Turning away'
  Examples from the first Christians
  Lessons to be learned
Children from believing homes
  Conversion or nurture?
  Covenant

The faith status of children

Having worked through part one of this book, the reader could be forgiven for asking the following question: 'If faith development is a natural and inevitable process, where does the idea of conversion fit in?' Indeed, it is the fear that a developmental understanding of faith rules out conversion which has made some evangelicals in the United States suspicious of James Fowler's work. In Britain, the contributions of Westerhoff and Fowler are less well known so the question is rarely asked.

Traditional evangelical assumptions

Among children's evangelists the traditional approach to evangelism is still the most widespread. I am not now talking about the *presentation* of the gospel or methods of communication. These have undergone far-reaching and radical changes in the last ten years with the introduction of drama, audio-visuals and videos. Christians in the sphere of children's work have not only kept up with the communications revolution of the secular world, but have also led the way in applying it to good effect in their work.

By 'the traditional approach', I am referring to the assumptions which lie behind the *structure* of the gospel message. Many evangelists assume that their goal is to bring children to a decision for Christ which corresponds to the kind of commitment asked of adults in evangelistic meetings and crusades. Consequently, a children's mission is typically geared up to a message which contains some or all of the following elements: (a) God the Creator; (b) Man the sinner; (c) Jesus the Saviour; (d) Our need to respond; (e) Jesus the friend. A standard five day mission would climax on the fourth or fifth day with a call to repentance, faith and a conscious decision to follow Christ.

At this point, it is important to understand what is *not* being said. I am not saying that every mission or event follows this pattern rigidly. Many will major on some aspect of Jesus' life rather than on a series of theological themes. But somewhere along the line these themes will emerge in some shape or form: certainly (b), (c) and (d) will for they constitute the core of the gospel. It would be hard to imagine evangelism which did not contain them. Neither am I saying that this traditional structure is bad. It is clearly not: God has used and blessed it for many years. I myself have spent the last thirteen years leading holiday missions based upon it.

However, if we are committed to child evangelism we must now ask what we can learn from the study of child development which will help us in our goal of bringing Christ to all ages. In particular we need to ask whether our model of conversion is not too adult and simplistic. For the structure of our evangelistic teaching remains specifically designed to evoke a response of faith which is (adult) decision-centred. This is why so much of a typical week's mission programme is geared to preparing children to hear about the atonement on day four or five: we hope that by first setting the scene for the Cross (the fact of sin, our need of forgiveness etc) in days one to three, and then by emphasizing the awfulness and costliness of Calvary, we will evoke a decision to accept Christ on the part of the child listener.

What is conversion?

We can approach this question from two directions. *Theologically*, we can ask what the Bible means by conversion and how this relates to the work of the Father, Son and Spirit. *Developmentally*, we can ask how the processes of child and faith development we have noted in part one of this book fit with a theological understanding of conversion. In the remainder of this chapter we shall look at both of these. We will begin by looking at the developmental views of faith and conversion: those of John Westerhoff and those of James Fowler.

John Westerhoff: Faith stages
John Westerhoff, writing from the perspective of what conversion means for someone who has grown up within the Christian faith, describes it as 'radical turning from "faith given" (through nurture) to "faith owned." '[2] In this he draws his model of the fourfold sequence of faith development we noted earlier: experienced (or given) faith, affiliative faith, searching faith and owned faith. Conversion comes as the bridge between stages three

and four. It is the 'act of surrender' by which a person gives himself wholly to God in a new and life-changing way. Two passages make this clear:

'Conversion experiences may be sudden or gradual, dramatic or undramatic, emotional or intellectual, but they always involve a major change in a person's thinking, feeling and willing – in short, in their total behaviour.'[2]

'Conversion . . . implies a reorientation in our thinking, feeling and willing; a moving from indifference or one form of piety to another. That is why conversion historically is only rarely a singular emotional outburst, a once-for-all dramatic occasion which can be dated and described. Rather, conversion is more typically a process by which persons are nurtured in a community's faith (the religion of the heart), go through the despair of doubt and the intellectual quest for understanding (the religion of the head), and at last, in late adolescence or early adulthood, experience illumination, certainty and identity.'[3]

John Westerhoff: Faith stages

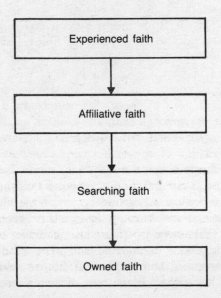

Experienced faith

↓

Affiliative faith

↓

Searching faith

↓

Owned faith

In Westerhoff's view, conversion is the outcome of both a moment and a process. The process of development comes to a head in the momentary act of surrender when the individual renounces self and gives everything to Christ. At that point he moves from a faith given to him largely by others to a faith which is appropriated and held for himself. 'Their faith' becomes 'his faith.' He has reached the stage of owned faith.

Differences with the classic evangelical model
So far, this fits with the classic evangelical model of conversion. But there are significant differences.

1. Westerhoff insists that conversion can never be separated from what has gone before. The life history of the convert is the soil out of which faith grows. The nurturing process of the preceding years is all important:

> 'Conversion . . . is never an isolated event devoid of all elements of nurture. Nurture and conversion are a unified whole.'[4]

2. Westerhoff locates the point of conversion overwhelmingly in late adolescence or early adulthood. This is no accident. His developmental structure requires that the sequence of faith stages must be gone through before conversion can take place. By definition, the act of surrender must come as the result of dissatisfaction with former affiliative faith and the desire to find something personally meaningful. This cannot happen until adolescence at the earliest.[5]

Implications of Westerhoff's analysis
Whether we agree or not with Westerhoff's analysis (especially with his association of conversion with adolescence), it carries some radical implications for children's evangelism. The most serious of these is the question of whether we can rightly speak at all of conversion before adolescence. On Westerhoff's scheme, it would seem that we cannot, since true conversion presupposes searching and surrender which are characteristics of adolescence and adulthood rather than childhood. The kind of sequence which culminates in the intellectual despair and desperation described by Westerhoff is not part of the childhood phases of

development in any sense. Neither intellectually nor emotionally is a pre-adolescent ready or capable of the reactions and responses involved in conversion as defined by the Westerhoff model.

Preaching the gospel to children

What, then, are we doing when we preach the gospel to children? I think on Westerhoff's logic we are doing several things which might best be described as pre-conversional. Firstly, we are *sowing seed for the future*. Children who hear the gospel may not yet be ready for the act of surrender and the stage of owned faith but they can store away the truth for the time when it will become relevant. A ten year old child who attends a holiday mission may find five or six years later that in the midst of his searching he recalls what he learned about Jesus at the mission. Now it becomes real for the first time. The meaning for which he has been searching suddenly (or slowly) clicks into place. The seed has come to fruit.

Secondly, we may be *persuading a child simply to switch his affiliation*. If we remind ourselves of the development models we shall recall that juniorhood and early adolescence constitute a period of affiliation. Children adopt beliefs which are those of the crowd or other influential persons such as parents. It is unlikely, given what we know about the structure of child development, that a junior child who comes along to a mission or Sunday school will be converted in the adult sense of making an independent decision to reorientate his life. This requires a more integral approach than children are generally capable of. What is much more likely is that the child who appears to make a decision for Christ at a mission, club or Sunday school has decided to start a new affiliation. This need not be a matter of insincerity: the desire to give his loyalty to a new group (the mission, church or whatever) can represent a genuinely heartfelt act. The giving of loyalty and the finding of meaning in a new group (particularly one which is not generally popular) is the central and greatest act of sincerity a child can make at this stage. It represents a powerful act of commitment.

But the meaning of such a commitment may lie in affiliation to the complex of persons and beliefs which make up the group, rather than to a personal acceptance of a set of truths. Sometimes this may include a powerful individual faith in the person of Jesus, sometimes a commitment to the shared faith of the group. We should not frown upon such group faith or regard it as inferior. Commitment to the group is often the highest form of commitment a child can make outside his or her immediate family relationships. We should not be looking for responses which are characteristically adult but for those which are realistically appropriate to child development.

This goes a long way to explaining two things common among children's missions and clubs. On one hand there are frequently large numbers of children who make professions of faith or want Jesus to be their friend; but on the other hand there is often a high subsequent drop-out rate. Children who were initially full of enthusiasm fall away. Those who have been faithful in attendance become less regular. Others are never seen at all between missions. (This is especially true of church-based missions which run every summer.) When this happens it is tempting to think that the child or children in question never really made a commitment of faith. 'If they were really disciples,' we say to ourselves, 'they would not have fallen off. Therefore they must never have been true Christians in the first place.'

The fact is that they probably never were – that is, as long as being a true Christian is defined in terms of an adult conversion experience. But my point is that this is the wrong standard by which to judge. The question is not whether they were ever genuinely converted but what kind of faith stage were/are they at? Many children who affiliate to a Christian group as the result of a mission move on to discover new affiliations after a time. This is not a deliberate renunciation of Christ: it is merely a part of the normal process of development. 'Taking Jesus as my friend,' then, often means, 'Finding new friends who also want to join this group' (in which case the spiritual formula used by the evangelist to denote acceptance of Christ functions like the enrolment oath of Brownies or Girl Guides – it signifies acceptance into the new affiliation). Or it may mean, 'I accept as true the beliefs this group holds as important and want to join it.' (The problem with this is that it is hard to know what the notions of acceptance and belief mean to a child in this situation.) Or it may mean, 'I like what I have found in this group and the people who run it and am therefore prepared to do what they want in order to belong.' If this means saying a prayer of repentance and faith in Jesus, then unless the child is an outright atheist he will happily say such a prayer. Again, we must not fall into the trap of supposing that it might not be genuine. The notion of hypocrisy is essentially adult. Within the framework of understanding and commitment which govern the affiliative stage, there will be very few children who (provided the cost of discipleship has been properly explained) will say they want to take Jesus as friend if they do not mean it.

Thirdly, when we evangelize we may be *triggering a child's movement from one stage of faith to another*. The fourteen year old who hears the gospel may for the first time in his life be faced with ultimate questions of life and death which lead on to the searching stage. But this will not always be so. It is not easy to trigger ultimate questions when a group is comfortably off and has never experienced hardship or grief. Such is the nature of modern life that many teenagers are able to coast along on the cushion of prosperity and security afforded by the affluent society. Many others, however, are experiencing the harsh side of this economic climate, and grow up with insecurity as a part of daily life. Nevertheless, when the questioning, searching stage is reached (and this may not be till the twenties or thirties), a person who has heard the gospel as a teenager or child will frequently find himself going back to what he heard years before.

We need to be clear, finally, that each of the stages described by Westerhoff is a stage of *faith*. It is not a question of a child's suddenly reaching faith at the final stage. All the way through, faith has been at work. As Westerhoff says:

'Let us never forget that . . . Christ died for us all, and no matter what style of faith we possess none are outside his redeeming grace.'[6]

Our evangelism, therefore, must be geared to enabling a child to *expand* such faith as he or she possesses.

In fact, statistics show that *conversion* in the Westerhoff sense is an overwhelmingly teenage experience. A series of six studies in the USA between 1899 and 1959 revealed that the average age of conversion ranged from 12.7 years to 16.6. Outside this range, the numbers of conversions were fewer and more scattered. It would appear that conversion is concentrated in the teenage years. As Cedric Johnson and Newton Malony have commented in their book *Christian Conversion: Biblical and Psychological Perspectives*, 'The sheer weight of statistical evidence lends credence to the notion that Christian conversion is a phenomenon of adolescence.'[7]

Does this mean that we can never talk meaningfully about the conversion of children? To answer this we must turn to another developmental model.

James Fowler: Faith content and conversion

James Fowler, while accepting Westerhoff's four stages of faith, offers a definition of conversion which is not confined to adolescence or adulthood. In his view, 'Conversion has to do with changes in the *contents* of faith.'[8] This can take place at any stage of development since there will always be some content to a child's faith (at least after infancy). It does not have to follow a period of searching or despair.

Fowler is able to adopt this definition of conversion because his original definition of faith is that of a set of meanings by which we give order and sense to our lives. It follows that we can change this set of meanings at any point and do not have to wait till adolescence or adulthood to do so. A child, for example, who has not been brought up to believe in Jesus may attend a mission or club in which the Christian faith clearly makes sense to the people who run it, whom he likes, and which therefore begins to make sense to him. As a result, he may decide to incorporate some of their beliefs and symbols into his own life. Time alone will tell whether these come to occupy the dominant place in his way of thinking but the point is that it is possible in principle that they will, even prior to adolescence.

On this basis the goal of evangelism must be to enable a child to accept a new set of meanings based on the idea of a relationship with Christ. These do not have to be understood in adult terms. The set of meanings can be geared to the appropriate stage of development so as to take account of the factors discussed in part one. In our speaking to junior age children, for example, we shall be concerned to couch this new set of meanings in concrete terms. In younger groups we might major on the idea of God as loving parent and so on.

According to Fowler, then, a person can be converted at any stage of life or faith. It is the change of content that matters rather than the stage of faith that has been reached. However, in addition to conversion thus defined, fowler identifies two other experiences commonly thought of as conversion but which, he maintains, should not be counted as such because they do not involve a change of content.[9]

The first of these he terms an *intensification experience*. This is a rather jargonistic way of describing an experience which deepens or renews previously held faith but which does not affect its contents. It amounts to an intense version of what has already been experienced. An example of this would be the adult who once was a fervent Christian but who has drifted away. He has not lost his faith but has become slack. He attends a church meeting and is renewed in faith and commitment. What has happened is not conversion since he has not discovered a new content of faith: he has merely come back to his first love.

The second experience does not have a convenient label. It involves being *catapulted from one faith stage to another by an event or experience*. But it does not involve any change in basic meanings or content. The movement, even though dramatic or sudden, takes place within the stream of faith in which the person was already situated. Thus a man who is stuck in the affiliative stage might be brought into the reflective stage by a tragedy within the family such as the death of his wife. As he reflects upon the meaning of death he realizes that his previous shallow views are no longer adequate and begins to search for a deeper faith which will enable him to cope. Merely parrotting the views of others ('She's at peace now. She can't suffer any more') is not enough. He has to find a set of meanings which will make sense of what has happened. He does so by moving on to the reflective stage within his previous tradition of belief. If he is a Christian he does not switch to Buddhism to provide the answers to his questions but goes more deeply into Christian teaching about the resurrection. This is but one example.

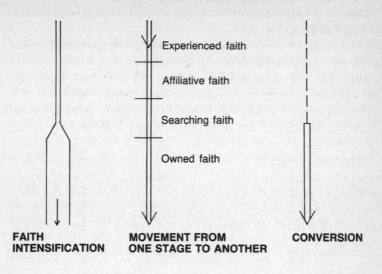

FAITH
INTENSIFICATION

MOVEMENT FROM
ONE STAGE TO ANOTHER

CONVERSION

Experienced faith

Affiliative faith

Searching faith

Owned faith

Fowler's five ways

From these three experiences – conversion, intensification and movement from one stage to another – Fowler argues that we can trace five ways in which conversion relates to stages of faith:

1. *Stage change without conversion*, as in the example above of the bereaved husband.

2. *Stage change that triggers conversion.* An example of this would be an adolescent who is in the affiliative stage but who begins to ask questions of meaning and purpose and in the process of moving into the reflective stage finds Christ at a Billy Graham Crusade.

3. *Conversion without stage change*, as in the case of an eleven year old from a humanist background who embraces the Christian faith but who remains at the affiliative stage.

4. *Conversion that triggers stage change.* Suppose the teenager above goes forward at a Billy Graham meeting along with his mates. None of them has a Christian background. Along with them, he changes the content of his faith but is still at the affiliative stage. But now suppose that this leads to his becoming more reflective as he reads the Bible and realizes that he has to commit his life fully to Christ. His conversion has triggered off a stage change.

5. *Conversion followed by blocked stage change.* An example of this would be someone converted to Christ at a children's camp or mission who never grew in maturity of faith as he or she got older. Such a person might hold a sincere and deeply felt faith but it would remain essentially as naive and undeveloped as at conversion. When confronted by doubt or questioning it either retreats into itself or collapses. Unfortunately, there are many such Christians in today's churches.

Conversion, then, is no simple matter. On Fowler's model, conversion does not refer so much to a sudden, dramatic experience as to a change in the meanings by which we order our lives, whether these come from faith in Christ or some other creed or commitment. This may involve a single, powerful experience or it may not.

Integration

However, we have to be clear on one further point: do we follow Westerhoff's definition of conversion or Fowler's? Westerhoff would seem to rule out child conversion whereas Fowler would seem to rule it in.

This divergence may not be as serious as first sight suggests. If we compare the two, we see that Westerhoff stresses the *attitude* of conversion while Fowler stresses the *content*. These need not be mutually exclusive. The content of Christian conversion must be faith in Christ. The adult or child who seeks Jesus must come to the point of giving himself or herself into his hands and asking Christ to rule his life. Westerhoff (I think) would be uneasy with this in the case of children because the searching phase which precedes the act of surrender presupposes characteristics that lie beyond childhood. Fowler, on the other hand, does not lay so much emphasis upon surrender and therefore can incorporate conversion within early stages of faith.

The answer may lie in broadening the notion of surrender to

take into account the characteristics of childhood. While it may be true that children do not have the capacity to go through the reflection and doubt at the heart of the searching stage, they nevertheless are capable of giving themselves to Jesus within the limits set by affiliative faith. The ten year old who enjoys a mission and wants to join the Jesus gang may still grasp that he is taking a step of commitment. Good evangelism will always make clear that becoming a friend of Jesus means giving everything over to him. Even if the child interprets this to mean that he must trust and obey the leaders of the Jesus gang, this still represents an act of surrender.

We must accept that both Fowler and Westerhoff offer valuable insights into conversion and that whilst there are some differences between them, we are best served by incorporating insights from both. It is impossible, however, to consider conversion solely in terms of developmental models. Conversion is a *theological* term and must be analysed theologically. Our next stop, therefore, will be the New Testament.

The New Testament and conversion

What does the New Testament mean by conversion? We can approach this in two ways. The first is to examine the terminology used by New Testament writers to speak of conversion. The second is to look at some key examples of conversion from the experience of the first Christians. As we do both of these we shall begin to see how theology and models of development can meet.

'Turning away'
The most common Greek word for conversion is *epistrepho*. Literally translated it means 'turning' or 'turning away'. Employed by the writers of the New Testament it takes on a threefold theological significance:

Firstly, it signifies a *'fundamental turning of the human will to God*, a return home from blindness and error to the Saviour of all.' It is not simply a matter of being sorry for the old way of life but a deliberate and heartfelt determination to change. Moreover, it is a recognition that such change can come about only by wholeheartedly turning to Christ. The person who is genuinely converted acknowledges that he cannot serve God by himself: his human will can always be bent by temptation and sin. Only by a surrender to Christ and a life lived in the power of grace can the convert find a true turnaround.

Secondly, *epistrepho* points to *a change in lordship*. Before conversion, human beings are under the temporary lordship of Satan (Eph 2:1–2). Without realizing it we follow his ways, live according to his dictates and are controlled by his power. We are in his kingdom of darkness whether we like it or not. But in Christ, God has triumphed over Satan. When we are converted we find a new lord – Jesus Christ who grants us perfect freedom within his kingdom of light. Conversion therefore means a total change in allegiance.

Thirdly, *epistrepho* indicates *a complete transformation of life in all respects*. Conversion does not lead to a chipping away at the edges of the former sinful self but to a radical remaking of every dimension. This is only possible in the power of the Holy Spirit. Left to ourselves we might long for radical change but only the Spirit can achieve such a transformation. Conversion is both brought about and sustained by God's Spirit. It is a supernatural work.

Theologically, then, conversion is God's act from beginning to end. This may seem to conflict with the emphasis of faith development models but in reality it does not. For God's grace flows both through natural (God-created) channels and through the momentary intervention of the Holy Spirit. We can therefore say that the development of faith through stages over time and the immediate crisis of conversion arise from the same source – the living God.

Examples from the first Christians

When we turn to the experience of conversion among the first believers, we find the same process at work. The book of Acts records five incidents of individual conversions:

1. Paul: Acts 9 (see also Gal 1 and Rom 7).
2. The Ethiopian Eunuch: Acts 8.
3. Cornelius: Acts 10.

4. Lydia: Acts 16.
5. The Philippian Jailer: Acts 16.

Although examination reveals that each of these conversions was unique, a certain pattern emerges.

The role of scripture
The first and most important element in this is the *role of scripture* in preparing a convert or evoking a sense of need. Paul is the most obvious case since he had been well versed in the law and the prophets as a Pharisee. But he was blind to their true meaning with regard to Christ. Once he had encountered the risen Lord, however, his knowledge was revolutionized. Under the creative inspiration of the Spirit, he was able to build a Christ-centred theology on the foundation of his deep knowledge of the Old Testament.

The scriptures were also vital for the others. The Ethiopian eunuch had been reading and meditating on Isaiah 53 when Philip appeared. Philip's exposition of how Jesus fulfilled the role of suffering servant opened his eyes and he was converted. As far as Cornelius is concerned, Luke makes it clear that 'he and all his family were devout and God-fearing'. It is quite likely that this involved some awareness of the Old Testament. Certainly Peter in Acts 10:42 was preaching the gospel. In Lydia's case, her scriptural knowledge seems to have derived from the apostles, although she may have had some prior awareness. Luke records that when Paul and the others visited Philippi, they spoke with her and other devout women at a place of worship by the river. Given what we know from elsewhere about Paul's expositions of scripture in similar situations, we can deduce that the scriptures had a definite role in triggering Lydia's conversion and may well have been influential before. This leaves us with the jailer. There is no indication about his level of scriptural awareness prior to his conversion but from the account in Acts 16 we do know that following the earthquake Paul and Silas 'spoke the word of the Lord to him and all that were in his house.' We can therefore discern a pattern in these five conversions which includes a pivotal role for the scriptures.

The work of the Holy Spirit

The second factor is the *work of the Holy Spirit*. Paul is not explicit about the role of the Spirit in his conversion but it is implicit in his statement that God 'was pleased to reveal his Son' to him (Gal 1:15–16). Since we know that the Spirit is God's chosen agent of revelation, it follows that what Paul is describing is the work of the Spirit. In the Ethiopian's case, however, the entire incident is explicitly surrounded by the Spirit: Philip is told by the Spirit to join the eunuch. The man then sees the truth and is baptized. Finally, Philip is taken away by the Spirit. The role of the Spirit could hardly be more pronounced. Cornelius' experience is different yet again. His conversion is accompanied by the gift of the Spirit and speaking in tongues (Acts 10:44–46). This should not be taken as a definitive sequence for all conversions since its purpose was to show that both conversion and the Holy Spirit were for the Gentiles as well as the Jews (see Acts 11). Nevertheless, it is clear that God was demonstrating that conversion must not be regarded as an act of the human will but had to be understood as something which could only take place under the impulse of the Spirit.

A preceding period of questioning

A third element we must notice is that in all but one case (the jailer), *the crisis of conversion was preceded by a period of questioning, inquiry or doubt*. Paul's experience on the road to Damascus seems to have come at the end of a time of inner conflict in which he had instigated the stoning of Stephen and had renewed his onslaught upon the Christians. It might be thought that these were signs of determination rather than conflict, but Paul's fanaticism betrayed the classic characteristics of insecurity and fear. This is reflected in his account of Jesus' words to him on the road: 'Saul, Saul, why do you persecute me? It hurts you to kick against the goads' (Acts 26:14 RSV). Similarly with the eunuch, Cornelius and Lydia: all were God-fearers of one kind or another and all were searching for truth.

The pattern that emerges, therefore, is one in which the scriptures, the Spirit and a period of searching all play a part in conversion to Christ. It should be added (although we do not have space to go into this here) that a further general factor was the incorporation of the new converts into the Christian community.

Lessons to be learned

There are four lessons for children's evangelism we should learn from these accounts.

Firstly, *conversion is from beginning to end the work of God*. We can never speak of it as a purely human act. At every stage God is involved even where apparently human processes are at work.

Secondly, *God works through such processes as he himself has ordained*. With the exception of Paul, it was the combination of the Spirit's direct activity within the convert and the God-guided messenger delivering the word through the human process of speech that brought the convert to faith. The function of the evangelist is therefore crucial.

Thirdly, *God spoke to each convert as a person with a personal faith history*. Each one had come to a point where previous beliefs were no longer adequate. Only Christ could give new meaning. In other words, these converts had already gone through a series of faith stages before they were ripe for conversion. This supports rather than rules out the recognition of faith stage development in the process of conversion.

Fourthly, *we must be cautious about applying adult models of conversion to children*. It is significant that nowhere in Acts do we find an account of child conversion. The most we can say is that the accounts point to how God acts towards adults and that by implication he acts similarly towards children. But even here we are speaking theologically: namely that we must reckon that the first three lessons above apply to children as well as adults. But what the Acts cases do not do is to provide a technique or a blueprint for converting children as if they were mini-adults.

Children from believing homes

Discussion of conversion brings us to the question at the centre of much recent debate among children's and family evangelists: how should we view the spiritual status of children from Christian families? Are they to be counted as members of the kingdom until they opt out? Or do they become members only when they consciously opt in by choosing Christ?

Conversion or nurture?

Much ink has been expended on this issue, and for good reason: our whole attitude to evangelism among children and families depends upon a clear view of our aim. Put bluntly, are we concerned with conversion or nurture? John Inchley makes a telling point when he says: 'It is sad to hear Christian parents declaring – "John is saved, though Mary isn't, and we are not quite sure about Bill." '[10]

This kind of conversation goes on regularly in Christian households. It is based on the view that no child, even from a believing background, can be counted as a member of God's kingdom until he or she has made an open and conscious declaration of faith. It would seem that the faith of parents counts for nothing.

Such a view has serious implications for the message Christian parents and workers give to children. The aim becomes evangelism rather than nurture. Everything is geared up to conversion. It is assumed that the child of Christian parents needs to 'get saved' in exactly the same way as would a child from an unbelieving home. The pastoral consequences of this can be horrific as the child senses that he can only please his parents by going through some 'conversion' experience which somehow makes him acceptable to them and to God. It is hardly surprising that later years see so many casualties of faith.

The saddest part, however, is that none of this is necessary. Both theologically and pastorally, children from Christian homes can be affirmed as members of the kingdom until they choose to reject their birthright.

Covenant

To understand this, we have to go back to scripture and the notion of family solidarity. We have seen how the faith of a believing parent (usually the head of the household in biblical times) counted as faith for the family as a whole. Like an umbrella it 'covered' them all. Whether or not individual members held the same belief as the parent, they were all counted by God as members of the convenant relationship established through the parent's faith.[10]

This can be seen in the Old Testament's view of covenant. In Genesis 17, we find God entering into a covenant with Abraham. The term covenant means 'promise' or 'agreement'. It was a common means of expressing and sealing a relationship in the Middle East in Old Testament times so that we find covenants between rulers of nations as a way of regulating their affairs.

The covenant between God and Abraham consisted of a twofold promise: that God would pledge himself to Abraham and his descendants and that they would pledge themselves to God. As a result, God would bless them by giving them the promised land and his protection. So it was that Israel came to see itself as a covenant people, chosen by God and called to a special relationship with him. 'I will be your God and you will be my people' became the watchword of the nation (Lev 26:12).

The basis of the covenant was God's grace. The covenant originated with God and the promise was held out by him. It did not depend upon faith for its *inception* although it had to be *received* by faith. So on the one hand God's promise came to Abraham 'out of the blue' (Gen 12:2–3) but, on the other, Abraham responded in faith. As Genesis makes clear, 'Abraham believed the Lord, and he credited it to him as righteousness' (Gen 15:6).

In Old Testament theology, Abraham came to represent Israel. So the nation as a whole was offered the covenant. Moreover, this was not confined to adults who had made an open profession of faith in our modern sense. It applied to all who were born as Israelites. Moreover, it applied to children.

This was emphasized in the rite of circumcision which was not simply a ritual but a sign established and commanded by God to show inclusion within the covenant. God's words to Abraham made this clear: 'You are to undergo circumcision, and it will be the sign of the covenant between me and you' (Gen 17:11). Thus Genesis 17:12 is explicit that *children* were to receive the sign of covenant acceptance: 'every male who is eight days old must be circumcised, including those born in your household or bought with money from a foreigner – those who are not your offspring.'

This is a profound testimony to three theological truths. Firstly, it shows that *the covenant relationship does not depend on faith but upon grace*. Otherwise eight day old infants could not have been included. Had acceptance by God depended upon their active individual faith, they would have been excluded from the household of God.

Secondly, it underlines the fact we have already noted: that *the faith of parents covers other members of the household*. This is the significance of the second half of verse 12: even those who are not blood relatives but are nevertheless part of the household are to be circumcised as a sign that they too are included in the covenant. In a home where there is at least one believing parent, it is his or her faith which counts for the rest until they deliberately reject God.

Thirdly, circumcision indicated that *children were to be treated as would-be believers rather than as unbelievers*. The rights and privileges of the covenant relationship were theirs. There could be no question of their being treated as outsiders: they were counted as insiders until they excluded themselves from God's blessing.

This pattern of relationship (though not the external sign of circumcision) was carried over into the New Testament. As we have seen, the conversion of the Philippian jailer and of Crispus fits the notion of covenant solidarity.

The implication for us is clear: we must count children of Christians as members of God's kingdom until such time as they refuse God's covenant promise. This means that it becomes more fitting to think of nurture than evangelism for such children. They have to be encouraged to *appropriate* the blessing they already possess by virtue of their status as covenant children. Once we realize this we free ourselves as parents and evangelists from the enormous pressure to bring about some kind of conversion experience for children who, theologically, are already accepted by God. No less importantly, we also liberate our children from fear, allowing them to become what God has made them: heirs of his covenant promise in Christ.

CONCLUSION

We have seen in this chapter that conversion must be studied *both* from the standpoint of faith development theories *and* from the standpoint of scripture. This is not always an easy match but if we are to be open to insights from both, we must be ready to engage in some tough reasoning. Without such reasoning we run the risk of missing vital truths which can shape our practice of evangelism and our understanding of nurture.

NOTES TO CHAPTER 7

1. John Westerhoff III, *Will Our Children Have Faith?* New York: Seabury Press, 1976, p 39.
2. Westerhoff, as above, p 98.
3. Westerhoff, as above, p 39.
4. Westerhoff, as above, p 39.
5. Though Westerhoff makes it clear that all stages of faith are to be counted within the scope of redemption.
6. Westerhoff, as above, p 99.
7. C Johnson & H N Malony, *Christian Conversion: Biblical and Psychological Perspectives*, Grand Rapids: Zondervan 1982, p 45.
8. James Fowler, *Stages of Faith*, New York: Harper & Row, 1981, p 281.
9. Fowler, as above, pp 285–286.
10. John Inchley, *All About Children*, Eastbourne: Coverdale, 1976, p 13.
11. For a detailed exposition of covenant theology, see L Berkhof, *Systematic Theology* London: Banner of Truth 1966 edn pp 262–304. Also C Brown (ed), *The New International Dictionary of New Testament Theology* vol 1, Exeter: Paternoster 1975 pp 365–376. Both show how, despite crucial differences between the old and new covenants, there is an essential continuity.

8
Those we teach

Children in context

A review of the idea of 'family' as a context for ministry to children:

Rediscovering the family
The family in society
In the Old Testament
In the New Testament
Children and families first?
1. *The church as the context for family life*
2. *The church as a model for family life*
3. *The church as an alternative family*

Rediscovering the family

The church in recent years has witnessed an upsurge in emphasis upon the family. We have had a variety of activities and services oriented towards family life: family service, family communion, family worship, family days. There are many reasons for this: a determination to hold fast to the family in the face of rapid social change; a realization that in the new housing estates of suburbia the best way to win interest (and hopefully faith) is through a family-centred strategy; a concern to get away from the image of religion as 'for women and kids' only; a rediscovery of the biblical emphasis upon the importance of the household as a place of nurture and growth. All these have been contributory factors in what might be called 'the family movement'.

This has sometimes led to rash and superficial assumptions. The most common of these has been the belief that when scripture speaks of family it means the same thing as the modern two-parent, two-child family, commonly known as the *nuclear family*. As we shall see, the biblical understanding is far removed from this distinctively modern view.

A second assumption has been that the local church must organize its worship, evangelism, teaching and social life around the needs of the nuclear family. The result is that many congregations function almost entirely as if what is good for the nuclear family is good for everyone else, irrespective of age, maturity and spiritual need. At its worst, this can make those who live apart from their wider families – such as the single and elderly – feel excluded. And however much the leaders of the church say the opposite, the effect of structures and worship which are predominantly aimed at the family can leave others feeling lonely failures.

So what is an appropriate theology of the family from which to develop pastoral and evangelistic practice?

The family in society

In the Old Testament

The family as a unit of kinship has provided the bedrock of

human society throughout history. But this kinship has been expressed in different forms from culture to culture and age to age. In biblical times, for example, it took the form of what is known as the *extended family*. Within this, there were several nuclear families containing husbands, wives and children, spanning several generations from great grandparents to great grandchildren. In addition, slaves and resident employees were counted as part of the family.

We can best illustrate this by a fictional example. Suppose Seth to be a forty year old man with a wife and four children. He is the eldest brother of five. In modern terms, this would be regarded as a family in itself. If we were to speak of Seth's family we would be understood as meaning his wife and their children.

Now imagine Seth in Old Testament society. If we spoke of his family, we would mean his wife and children, the wives and offspring of any of his sons who were married, his brothers and their wives and children, his parents and possibly grandparents, his cousins and their children, his slaves and their kin, his servants and his employees. This extended family would be economically self-supporting and bound to the collective security of the clan and the tribe. In every conceivable way, therefore, it would be supported and buttressed from within and without. It was an extremely stable structure in which to rear children.

The Old Testament family

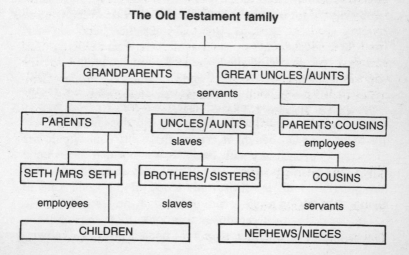

It was within the family, moreover, that each individual found his identity. He did not regard himself, nor was he regarded by others, as an individual apart from his household. So our imaginary Seth would be not merely Seth, but Seth son of Reuben, of the clan of Libni, of the tribe of Benjamin and so on. The notion of family and communal solidarity was all powerful.

This is a far cry from our modern concept of the nuclear family. Moreover, it contrasts heavily with the notion of a single-parent family, where the structures and bonds of the extended household have shrunk to vanishing point.

When we speak, then, of ministry to families arising from a biblical commitment to the family, we need to be very careful. Not only are the definitions of family very different, but in biblical societies (especially Israel) the family was a self-supporting economic, social and spiritual unit in itself. Those who call for a return to biblical patterns of family must recognize the very different world in which we live.

So far, we have had in mind mainly the Old Testament. What of the New?

In the New Testament

When we turn to the New Testament we see the idea of the household or family of God used in three distinct senses.

The whole church of God

The first was in relation to the whole church of God. Just as Israel had been described as the household of Yahweh (Num 12:7), so Christians as 'the new Israel' could rightfully regard themselves as the 'house of God' (Heb 3:2–6).

Why did the writer to the Hebrews use this metaphor? He did so because he thought it crucial that Christians should see themselves in continuity with Israel. It was not that they should copy Old Testament structures but that they should realize that through their faith in Christ they stood in the same kind of relationship to God and one another as had the Jews.

This carried with it certain implications. First and foremost, they had to understand that they were not a collection of individuals each going his or her own way but rather a community with a sense of family oneness, a household belonging to God. No less importantly, the same kind of obligations and bonds which had characterized families in the Old Testament must now characterize the Christian family. They might not be tied by bonds of blood but their unity in Christ laid upon them no less powerful obligations of love.

This meant, in turn, that two further features of the Old Testament structure were important. The first was the encouragement of worship and teaching. The household structure of Israel had played a crucial part in the process of religious and social nurture. In transferring the family metaphor to the early Christians, the writer to the Hebrews was making clear that they must be faithful to this.

Caring and solidarity

The second feature was the caring function of the household. In the Old Testament the family had been a place of refuge, affirmation and inclusion. The family (in the largest sense) was the place where the individual 'found the substance and experience of his status as a member of the covenant people of God.'[1] In times of trouble he could find support in the family. In times of rejoicing he could share his joy with his kin.

More than that, however, the Israelite household had provided support for those who were not members by blood but were slaves or servants. These were now counted as members of the extended family. In the same way the New Testament household of God was exhorted to care for those whose normal blood ties had been disrupted by one cause or another. Such believers were not to regard themselves as kin-less but were to be welcomed into their new family, the church. As Paul wrote in Ephesians 2:19, 'You are no longer foreigners and aliens but fellow-citizens with God's people and members of God's household.'

By encompassing not only kin but servants and employees, such solidarity bound all the members of the household into a tightly knit unit. The action of one became the action of all, particularly if that one was the head. When he, therefore, entered into an agreement or acted in some other way, the entire family was counted as having acted. As we shall see in a moment, it is important to keep this principle in mind when interpreting some key New Testament texts.

The local church

The images and responsibilities which applied to the church as a whole also applied to local congregations. This application was readily achieved since the first churches began as family households. As Christopher Wright has noted:

> 'The use of family and household imagery for the local Christian churches was, of course, greatly facilitated by the historical fact that many of them originated as converted households and actually met in homes.'[2]

This carried over into the New Testament. In several places we find that the conversion of the head of the house is held to count for the conversion of the entire family. In Acts 16, for example, we have a striking example of this with the Philippian jailer. He had been guarding Paul and Silas when an earthquake shook the prison and opened the doors. Fearing that the prisoners had escaped, the jailer was about to kill himself when stopped by Paul. When asked by the jailer what he must do to be saved, Paul's reply was significant: 'Believe in the Lord Jesus, and you will be saved – you *and your household*' (16:31).

This last phrase is important. Within a matter of hours all the household (which meant blood kin, servants and employees) were baptized. Now it is unlikely that each member had undergone a personal conversion experience in the way that the jailer had. The explanation which best fits our knowledge of family life in biblical times is that the faith of the head of household was counted on behalf of the others *as if it were their own*.

A second example follows only two chapters later (18:1–8). In Corinth Paul preached to the synagogue Jews. Luke notes that Crispus, the ruler of the synagogue, was converted along with his entire household. Again, it would be unusual that everyone in the household should have been converted at the same time. It would (on the principle of family solidarity) seem much more likely that Crispus' faith was held to determine that of his household. This has significant implications for modern ministry to families.

Children and families first?

What we have seen so far about the biblical concept of family is of great importance for our own evangelistic and pastoral strategy. Broadly speaking, we can speak of church and family under three headings.[3]

1. The church as the context for family life

The shift in modern societies away from extended to nuclear families has meant that families have frequently lacked support and help which in previous generations would have been supplied by blood kin. This has become increasingly true as families have become geographically more mobile. The modern equivalent of Seth's family might well no longer live in the same area (let alone under the same roof) but instead be scattered all over the country.

In this situation, the local church becomes the extended family. Its life and fellowship enable individual family units to find their identity within the collection of families gathered together under its umbrella. Faith comes to replace blood as the bond which holds people together. Moreover, as they live out their transformed and transforming relationships through Christ, they are knit together in faith and love. This has a feedback effect upon individual families as family life is affirmed and enriched.

A warning note must be sounded, however. A family-oriented church can easily become introverted. As families are built up, they can simply enjoy one another's support and fellowship without looking outwards. In the end, the church can become a family ghetto where its members come solely to enjoy the atmosphere of a cosy club. Such a church quickly becomes lukewarm in its prayer for those outside the fellowship and in its evangelistic thrust. Indeed, these are two vital indicators of the spiritual strength of the church family.

2. The church as a model for family life

An attractive family is one which demonstrates love and support. The same is true for the church. It is the quality of care and fellowship which convinces the outsider that there is something life-giving in the Christian faith. So it is that simply by acting as the family of God, the local church evangelizes – often without knowing it. By the same token, the qualities of integrity, honesty and love which characterize the church family will model to others what God's grace can achieve in any family's life. In saying this, we must not allow ourselves to get carried away with unrealistic idealism. For being a family, whether Christian or not, involves pain and conflict as individuals learn to live with one another. But within the church viewed as a family and within believing families which make up the church, the Spirit of Christ will bring a new quality of life and fellowship that will model the kingdom of God to outsiders.

3. The church as an alternative family

The fragmenting of kinship groups in modern times has meant that large numbers of single people now find themselves without the immediate bonds of a natural family. The single elderly, widows and widowers, the unmarried of all ages, those distanced from their families by work or circumstances all represent individuals who, for one reason or another, are cut adrift from the supportive structures of the nuclear family.

It is to these groups that the local church can minister as an alternative family. For many inner city churches this is precisely their role. An inner London vicar once described his church to me as 'a transit camp for young singles needing to be in London for a certain period of their lives.' In such circumstances, the church needs to be sensitive to the range of needs within it. What may be appropriate for suburbia where there are large numbers of nuclear families may be highly inappropriate for an inner city church where nuclear families are few and far between. In this situation, the family service (or perhaps better, family communion) must centre on the idea of the whole church as God's family, rather than on catering for the needs of nuclear families alone.

Similarly, even where there are numbers of families, the composition of the wider congregation must be taken into account in the development of the life and worship of the church. Myrtle Langley writes tellingly of her experience as a single person:

'It may come as a surprise to many that it is in the church, the community of faith which is the people of God, that single people, women especially, experience the most acute pain. In many churches, particularly within the evangelical tradition, the central worship event of the week is a "family service", sometimes little more than over-age, over-size Sunday school. Similarly, the main church organizations usually cater for "wives", "mothers", "couples", "children", "the under thirty-fives" and "the elderly"! What of the rest!'[4]

The church

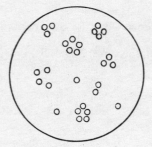

Context for family life

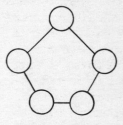

Model for family life

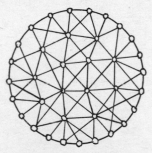

Alternative for family life

CONCLUSION

In the shifting social circumstances of our time, therefore, our understanding of the church as family must not focus on trying to copy the structure of either the extended or nuclear family, but on reproducing the *quality* of relationships which the biblical image of family evokes: loving, caring, fair, supportive and affirmative. These can characterize any fellowship whatever its age and marital profile. Where this happens, the concept of family can unify a congregation and contribute to the upbuilding of the local body of Christ.

NOTES TO CHAPTER 8

1. Christopher Wright, *Living as the People of God*, Leicester: IVP 1983, p 194.
2. Wright, as above.
3. I am grateful to my colleague Gordon Oliver for the structure of this section.
4. Myrtle Langley, *Equal Woman*, Basingstoke: Marshalls, 1983, p 169.

9
What we teach

Three issues in modern evangelism

The doctrine of the Trinity in relation to evangelism:

Father evangelism
Jesus evangelism
Spirit evangelism

The doctrine of the Trinity in relation to three key issues in modern evangelism:

ISSUE 1: The Fatherhood of God
Abba, Father
Must we speak of God only as Father?
The Old Testament
The New Testament
Evangelistic implications
For our message
For our approach

ISSUE 2: Why the Incarnation matters
Its centrality to Christianity
Incarnation and evangelism
A God who loves all he has made
A God who redeems all creation

Evangelism and the Trinity

If we were asked to give a simple definition of evangelism, what would we say? Preaching the gospel? Telling others about Christ? Bringing people to repentance and faith? In fact, most evangelism centres on the person of Jesus. His life and ministry are presented as a prelude to the most important part of his mission – his death. But we have to ask ourselves whether such an approach is adequate. For a truly biblical approach to children's, or any other, evangelism must begin with the foundation of Christian belief: not concentration on Christ alone but on the three persons of the Trinity – Father, Son and Holy Spirit. In this chapter we shall begin to see how the Trinity forms the essential structure of the gospel message and how the realization of this can revolutionize our approach to evangelism. We shall look at three approaches which concentrate on one member of the Trinity or another largely to the exclusion of the others. For clarity we shall call these: *Father* evangelism, *Jesus* evangelism and *Spirit* evangelism.

Father evangelism

A Father-centred gospel will reflect the qualities of God the Father but underplay the importance of the Son and the Spirit. So we may end up with a message that stresses the Creatorship of God and the love which he shows to his creatures in sustaining and strengthening them but which is decidedly weak on sin, repentance and the need for forgiveness through the Son. In addition, the Spirit may be presented as little more than an impersonal force.

The upshot of this will be to present a gospel message which is fuzzy. God's love will be affirmed but in such a way that it seems to embrace all people without condition or qualification. 'Surely,' it will be said, 'if God is the Creator of all people, he is their Father and they may rest secure in his hand.'

The great weakness of such a view is that it inevitably makes light of sin and devalues the death of Christ. Indeed, it is difficult to see (on some versions of it) why Jesus had to die at all. The strength of Father evangelism, however, is that it takes seriously the profound truth that God cares for the whole of his created order, not just those who have declared their allegiance to Christ. If this seems obvious, it needs to be remembered that throughout Christian history there have been plenty of groups which have denied the importance of the created world and even the human body, arguing instead that the Fall has corrupted creation and only the spirit can be made pure before God.

There are few today who would make such extreme claims but this attitude can still be found in weakened form. How often do we hear it said or implied that God is more concerned about the state of our souls or our 'spiritual' life than he is about our bodies? Or how much do we give the impression in our evangelism that relationship with God is essentially an inward thing – a meeting of his Spirit with ours? This kind of understanding is fundamentally at odds with the biblical view that God has created us as whole persons, not just spirits, and that in Christ we are redeemed as whole persons.

We can see, then, that while Father evangelism contains some important truths, to concentrate exclusively upon the Father without relating the person and work of the Father to that of the Son and Spirit leads to imbalance.

Jesus evangelism

If the danger of some Father evangelism is that it devalues the death of Christ, the danger of the purely 'Jesus' approach is that it stresses nothing else. At the heart of the gospel, of course, lies the message that 'Christ died for our sins and rose again on the third day.' But there is much more to say. We have not exhausted the New Testament teaching on Jesus merely by reference to the events of Good Friday. His death has to be set in a total theological context which involves the purpose of God for the whole world and the particular role of Christian believers within it. We dare not suppose that because we have spoken of the cross as God's way of dealing with sin and of the need for our response, we have done more than *begin* to understand why God sent his Son. Evangelism which treats the life of Jesus simply as a necessary prelude to the last twenty-four hours of his life is in serious danger of misleading its hearers. The answer to the question 'Why did Jesus die?' is not simply, 'To save us from our sins.' It is a great deal more.

A second weakness in Jesus evangelism lies in what happens within the continuing life of the believer after he or she has come to faith. A concentration upon Christ as the object of belief in the preaching of the gospel easily leads to worship which is centred only on the Son. Prayers are addressed to Jesus alone, thanksgiving is made to him alone for his giving of himself upon the cross, praise is focussed entirely upon the blessings imparted by the risen Christ, and the continuing life of the believer is portrayed as living only in obedience to the Son.

As with Father evangelism, this is not so much wrong as out of balance. Jesus understood his ministry in relation both to the Father and to the Spirit. He did not seek glory for his own sake but for the sake of his Father. Moreover, he proclaimed his coming as the revelation of the Father. Once we grasp this, we can see that to focus predominantly or exclusively upon Christ runs the risk of appearing to set the Son over and against the Father or simply to leave the Father out altogether.

Spirit evangelism
Many millions of Christians the world over have found a new richness of life in the renewal of the Spirit which has swept the church in recent years. Far from being feared, this is to be welcomed and rejoiced in. But this new-found emphasis upon the forgotten member of the Trinity should not blind us to some

of the problems it has brought in its wake. In evangelism there is the danger that the spectacular side of renewal may be seen as a substitute for a biblical understanding and experience of God as Father and Son as well as Spirit.

Put differently, it becomes easy to preach the gospel as a series of dramatic experiences such as healing, speaking in tongues and other signs and wonders. When these do not happen, it is thought that either the truth is not being proclaimed or that there is some inner fault of faith on the part of the hearers.

In the New Testament, however, the activity of the Holy Spirit is described in far wider terms than just dramatic happenings. Once more we have to develop our theology of the Spirit from a trinitarian standpoint. We must understand the Spirit's work as the outcome of the relationship of the Spirit to the Father and the Son. Only then will we be in a position to relate signs and wonders to the gospel as a whole.

I have stressed this because Spirit evangelism has in some quarters come to be seen as the antidote to the decline of Christian faith in a secular society. As the church has become less significant in the lives of most people and in society at large, so a school of thought has grown up which claims that the only way to convince an unbelieving and sceptical world of the truth of Christ is to demonstrate the power of God in dramatic ways. On this analysis, true evangelism only takes place when signs and wonders are present as demonstrations of the kingdom. So the gospel becomes less a matter of preaching repentance and faith and more a response to supernatural signs. Evangelism which is truly trinitarian, however, will provide a necessary corrective to this.

Where next?
So far the reader may wonder where children fit into all this. But while child evangelism raises its own set of questions which relate to childhood, it must be seen as part of evangelism as a whole. This is especially true on a theological level where it is sometimes supposed that there must be a child theology which is separate from that which is relevant for adults.

Such a view is misguided. It is true that the theology of the

Bible and of Christians through the ages has been cast in an adult mode. But that is not the same thing as saying that the biblical truth which adults need to hear is different in substance from that which children need to hear. It *is* the case that our presentation of the gospel must take account of what modern theories of child development tell us about the educational, psychological and social development of the child. But the truth which God has given us about himself – Father, Son and Spirit – remains true for all age groups not just for adults. The urgent task is to find a way of conveying it which does justice to the message and its hearers alike.

This brings us back to the Trinity. We have seen that it is possible to construct evangelistic approaches which concentrate exclusively or predominantly on only one or other person of the Trinity. But there is one further danger we must guard against. That is the assumption that this problem can be overcome simply by putting the three models side by side. Such an approach could be represented in the form of a diagram:

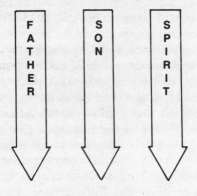

EVANGELISM

But this would be to miss the crucial point: the Trinity is not about three persons existing separately in parallel with a bit of overlap here and there. It is about the *continuous relationship* between Father, Son and Spirit. The diagram over the page illustrates this. At the core of our evangelism, whether it be addressed to children or adults, lies the profound interrelation of the three persons of the Godhead. This casts a wholly different light on much of what passes for evangelism today.

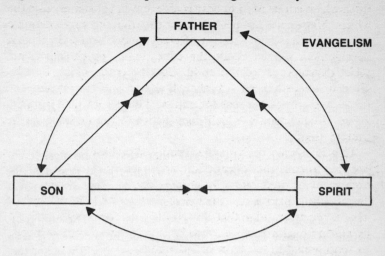

ISSUE 1: The fatherhood of God

In our discussion of Lee and Lizzie in part one, we noticed how important parental images are to the development of faith. But no less important is how we understand the parenthood of *God*. Ministry to children and families in contemporary society throws up a number of crucial questions about the fatherhood of God and the appropriateness of solely masculine language to describe God. Moreover, it raises questions about what kind of family ministry is most appropriate in a context of increasing divorce rates and one-parent families. It is crucial, therefore, that we examine ways in which the Bible approaches these issues and how this, in turn, can help us to minister more effectively.

Abba, Father
Professor Joachim Jeremias remarks that, 'No less than one hundred and seventy times in the Gospels we find the word "Father" for God on the lips of Jesus.' In John's Gospel alone, it occurs 109 times.[1]

When we probe a little more deeply, we discover two words

translated as 'father' in the New Testament. The most common is the Greek *pater*. This was the ordinary, everyday term used of earthly fathers. But to grasp its significance we have to remember that although the New Testament was written in Greek, Jesus spoke in Aramaic. Here the word for father was *abba*. This occurs in only three places: Mark 14:36, Romans 8:15, and Galatians 4:6. Scholars are agreed that the ideas contained within *abba* lie behind the New Testament's use of *pater*, but that there was something about Jesus' use of *abba* which both Mark and Paul felt it important to retain. We shall see in a moment what that was.

So when Jesus spoke of God as Father what did he mean? We must look first at the understanding of fatherhood prevalent in Jesus' day, then secondly, at the distinctive content that he gave this in relation to God.

The first point we must make is a negative one. The notion of fatherhood in New Testament times was not the sentimental idea common to our own society. 'Father' in Jesus' world was not the indulgent parent who can be manipulated by the sweet smile of his beloved offspring. He was, in fact, the absolute head of the household to whom the utmost respect was due. His word was law. For this reason, the codes of household behaviour laid down by the apostles for the first Christians stated explicitly that obedience to parents was a necessary sign of obedience to God. On the other side, parents had equally to treat their children with respect (see Col 3:20–21).

Nothing could be further from our modern child-centred view of parenthood. In this both father and mother exist for the sake of the child. The child's wishes (usually portrayed as needs) become the governing factor in the running of the household. So the entire lives of the parents become geared to a child-oriented lifestyle.

Yet this was simply not the notion with which Jesus worked. When he referred to God as Father he had in mind an attitude to fatherhood which addressed father not as 'daddy' but as 'dear father' – a much greater term of respect.

This is shown by the history of the word *abba*. Originally it was used to denote baby language. According to the Jewish rabbis, when a child was weaned, it learned to say *abba* (daddy) and *imma* (mummy). As times passed, however, *abba* ceased to be applied just to the language of babes and instead came to be used by older children and adults of their father. By the time of Jesus this process was complete: *abba* was no longer the childish term for father but the mark of respect. *Abba* then is a term of intimacy but not indulgence, of both response and respect.

So we are brought to the contexts in which God is addressed directly as *Abba*. There are only three of these and it is significant that all of them have to do with prayer.

Gethsemane

Mark 14:36 shows Jesus the Son face to face with his Father in prayer in Gethsemane. The crucifixion is only hours away. A few verses earlier Mark records Jesus as being 'deeply distressed and troubled' so that 'he fell to the ground and prayed that if possible the hour might pass from him' (33–35). In the midst of this, Jesus addresses God as *Abba*, dear Father. At the moment of inner torment his appeal is to the One who is both intimate yet powerful.

This, more than any other verse in the Gospels, underlines the inadequacy of translating *abba* simply as 'daddy'. It is inconceivable that the Son of God in the midst of his agony, on the eve of his death should have appealed to his heavenly Father in the tones of babyhood. We have here not the frightened child running to the arms of his safe protective daddy but the adult son bringing his fears to the father he loves and respects and who, he knows, loves and respects him in return. This implies a fundamental equality of relationship often overlooked in modern evangelism.

The outcome is obedience. The will of the Father is fulfilled in the Son. We should not make the mistake of supposing that Jesus somehow was coerced into death. As he declares in John 10:18, 'No one takes it [my life] from me, but I lay it down of my own accord.' Similarly, the Gospels make it clear that Jesus, as the incarnate second person of the Trinity, emerged from his agony in Gethsemane to embrace death of his own free will. As Jeremias observes, 'In Jesus' prayers *abba* is not only an expression of obedient trust but also at the same time a word of authority.'[2]

Adoption

Romans 8:15 and Galatians 4:6 speak of our right to call God *Abba* by virtue of our adoption as members of his family. Just as Christ is the Son of God, we are to regard ourselves as his brothers and sisters possessing the same right to address God as 'dear Father'. We are no longer slaves but heirs because God has given us the rights of sonship through his Son Jesus.

The enormity of this strikes home when we realize that nowhere in the Old Testament or in Jewish prayers at the time of Christ is God addressed directly as *Abba*. To the Jew it would have been disrespectful and familiar. That Jesus did so was revolutionary, but for his followers to do so was unbelievable. Who on earth (literally) possessed the right to speak to the sovereign of the universe in that way?

To address God as Father, then, whether as *Abba* or as *Pater* represents a step which is at the same time both familiar and awesome. It is not 'Daddy' but 'dear Father'. In doing so, we enter into the presence of one whom only the Son could initially address as Father but who has graciously welcomed us as fellow addressees alongside his Son. We speak to our Father, therefore, not in tones which imply he is taken for granted, but as those who recognize the unique combination of intimacy and reverence contained in the title we have come to know so well.

Must we speak of God only as Father?

The rise of feminism has forced us to ask searching questions about the way we speak about God. What does it mean to describe God in predominantly male terms? Can we continue to do so? Should God be thought of solely as masculine? These are not burning questions for most children's workers. But, as we shall see, they are nevertheless important questions because they affect the way we portray God to children.

Some feminist theologians have gone so far as to advocate the abandonment of male-only descriptions of God on the ground that they represent the products of a male-dominated biblical culture rather than definitive revelation from God. However, it is not necessary to go so far in a radical direction (which carries vast implications for our doctrine of scripture as well as our doctrine of God). For if we look carefully, we can see that the Bible itself contains pictures of God which are decidedly feminine and which must be put alongside those which are masculine. This enables us to respond to the criticism that scripture is inherently sexist.

It also enables us to set our understanding of family in a theological context. There is an odd paradox here. When we think of human families we invariably think in terms of mother, father and children (and sometimes grandparents). Yet when we apply family imagery to the Godhead, we nearly always focus exclusively on the maleness of God. We might just as well speak of human families only in terms of children and *fathers*.

This is usually presented in terms of imitating within earthly families the qualities of God the heavenly Father: fatherly love, fatherly steadfastness and reliability, fatherly strength, fatherly authority. These are seen as the characteristics and qualities which we must live out in our human families. It is the *fatherhood* of God which provides the controlling image for our understanding of what makes good family life.

Such an approach, however, does not go to the root of the issue. Our theology of the family should begin with our theology of God. So we are driven back to ask whether it is right to conceive of God in purely masculine terms or whether there is not also room for the feminine dimension.

A moment's reflection should make us think twice before applying only male images to the Godhead. After all, the norm which we set for human families includes both father *and* mother. We do not, as a rule, happily accept as best a structure containing only one parent. We stress the importance of both parents for the wholeness of family life. Ironically, we assume that if there is to be single parenting, it should usually be the mother.

This contrasts so heavily with a theological emphasis upon the fatherhood of God that we are given pause for thought. After all, if we regard both parents as crucial to a holistic view of the human family, should we not also look to see what this implies about the Godhead? If all creation (including the human family) is a reflection of God, then what within the Godhead corresponds to human motherhood as well as fatherhood? Perhaps we should be asking 'whatever happened to the motherhood of God?'[3]

To raise this is not to indulge in theological trendiness or liberalism. It is simply to follow through a series of legitimate questions that arise once we begin to reflect on the meaning of God as the heavenly parent. Fortunately we are encouraged in this by the fact that scripture itself contains hints and clues pointing in the same direction.

The Old Testament

We find the first clue in the opening chapters of Genesis. In chapter 1, God commands that humanity is to be made after his own image (v 26). How is this image to be expressed? The answer is in the creation of male and female, not in the creation of male alone. Thus the writer records: 'So God created man in his own image, in the image of God he created him; *male and female* he created them' (v 27).

The image of God, and therefore God himself, consists then in both male and female. Since God expresses himself through his image, we need to speak not just of his fatherhood but of his motherhood, whilst recognizing the predominance of the father image in scripture.

Other clues can be found scattered throughout the Old Testament. For instance:

Psalm 17:8	God the mother bird shelters and protects her young.
Psalm 22:9	God the midwife brings the baby to birth and watches over it as it suckles at its mother's breasts.
Isaiah 49:15	God the mother suckles the baby.
Isaiah 66:13	God the mother comforts the child Israel (see also Ps 131:2).

Equally significant are references alluding to God in both masculine *and* feminine terms:

Psalm 123:2	God is both master and mistress of servants.
Isaiah 42:13–14	God is a man of war *and* a woman in labour.

But most telling is Deuteronomy 32:18. This is not well translated in either the Good News Bible or the New International Version; the Revised Standard Version is clearer. Speaking of himself, God says: 'You were unmindful of the Rock that begot you, and you forgot the God who gave you birth.' Peter Craigie in his commentary on the passage makes the female image even more explicit by adding the words 'in pain' after 'gave you birth'. He believes this renders the Hebrew more accurately.[4] The picture, therefore, is of God who is both father ('the Rock that begot you') and mother ('who gave you birth in pain'). We could not move further away from an image of God which is purely masculine.

The New Testament

The New Testament contains imagery similar to that of the Old, albeit not quite so plentiful. As we shall see, however, this is partly replaced by a theology of Christ which incorporates feminine aspects.

Just as in the Old Testament, the New contains birth-giving and suckling metaphors. Perhaps the best-known is from John 3:5, where Jesus tells Nicodemus: 'Unless a man is born of water and the Spirit, he cannot enter the kingdom of God.' Here, however, the maternal role is given to the Holy Spirit. This immediately broadens out our application of the family image to the Godhead. Nevertheless, the maternal imagery is there. As Jesus says: 'Flesh gives birth to flesh, but the Spirit gives birth to spirit' (v 6). A little further on, Jesus speaks of being 'born of the Spirit' (v 8).

Similarly, Peter reminds believers that their relationship to God is like that of babes to their mothers:

'For you have been born again, not of perishable seed, but of imperishable, through the living and enduring word of God. . . Therefore . . . like newborn babies, crave pure spiritual milk, so that by it you may grow up in your salvation, now that you have tasted that the Lord is good.' (1 Pet 1:23; 2:2)

This passage is important in two respects. Firstly, by using the phrase 'imperishable seed', Peter is drawing attention to the analogy between the fathering process involved in ordinary human reproduction and the divine fathering process by which Christians are born anew. As birth in the flesh is brought about by the implantation of male seed, so spiritual birth is accomplished by the seed of the heavenly Father. This seed is God's word. But, secondly, we are reminded no less firmly of God's *motherly* activity in breast-feeding newborn Christians. Just as a baby craves its mother's milk, so we are to long for spiritual milk, especially as we have now tasted the milk from God's breasts.

This startling picture has usually been neglected out of a concern to emphasize the fragility of newborn believers and their need to be nourished carefully. The passage has been used predominantly, therefore, in a pastoral sense. This is appropriate for pastoral purposes, but we must not overlook the theology of God which is contained here: namely that he must be described in both masculine and feminine images. Indeed, without both, the text does not make sense. This brings us to Christ. The best-known reference to the feminine dimension of God in Jesus is in Matthew 23:37. Here Jesus laments the future destruction of Jerusalem by comparing himself to a mother hen:

'O Jerusalem, Jerusalem, you who kill the prophets and stone those sent to you, how often I have longed to gather your children together, as a hen gathers her chicks under her wings. . .'

The implication is obvious: Jesus loves with a mother-love that longs to protect and safeguard its own. The fact that Jesus was a man does not obliterate the femininity of God in him.

The last consideration we must give to the New Testament is a little more complicated. However, it is of such importance that it cannot be overlooked. Its starting point is the personification of Wisdom found in both Old and New Testaments and (no less importantly) in the Jewish religious literature of the period between the testaments.

This may seem odd to us because we think of wisdom as an abstract quality. We say a person has wisdom or is wise but we do not think of wisdom itself as a person. The Bible is quite different. It is true that wisdom is thought of in places as a characteristic of a particular figure such as Solomon (see 1 Kings

3:28). But in those books of the Old Testament compiled after the exile, it becomes possible to speak of Wisdom (with a capital letter) as if it were a person rather than an abstraction.

A key passage is Proverbs 8. It is too long to reproduce here but a number of points stand out:

1. Wisdom is portrayed as the one who reveals, and teaches about, God.
2. Wisdom is just and righteous (20).
3. Wisdom has been at God's side since before creation (22–30).
4. Wisdom was God's craftsman in the work of creation (30).

Two things are noteworthy. Firstly, the characteristics ascribed to Wisdom in Proverbs are precisely those identified with the Word of God (Christ) in the opening chapter of John's Gospel. And secondly, Wisdom both in Proverbs and elsewhere is described as 'she'.

We have, therefore, a description of Wisdom as feminine and, at the same time, an identification of the *nature and activity* of Wisdom with Christ. It follows that the *feminine characteristics* of Wisdom are also to be seen in the nature of Christ. This is striking evidence for taking seriously the feminine dimension of the Godhead.

To sum up then, we find that both Old and New Testaments contain powerful hints concerning the feminine aspect of God. This is suggested by the image of God in humanity, the motherly metaphors of both testaments, and Wisdom theology applied to Christ. In the light of these, we must now look to some positive implications for evangelistic ministry.

Evangelistic implications

For our message
If we take the arguments of the previous pages seriously, the primary effect upon our message will be that we stop portraying God in male macho terms. Part of our problem is that we have come to identify God with a particular understanding of masculinity. But this itself is conditioned by what we in western society have defined as masculine: physical toughness, strength, power,

forcefulness, and so on. We have to struggle hard not to think of God (particularly in the Old Testament) as a kind of cosmic Rambo: full of power, action and violence, storming all over the place to impose his will. It is at this point that we need to remember the feminine images.

I am not supposing this re-evaluation of our message about God will be easy. For children, especially, reared on a diet of television action in which good men are macho men, the transition to a God who *is* powerful but not capricious will be difficult. But if we are to be true to scripture, we have no option. We *must* develop a theology appropriate to children which portrays both the strong power of God and his tender care.

For our approach

One of the most perplexing problems facing those involved in family and children's ministry is to know what to do with the fatherhood of God. This arises not so much from theological as from sociological problems. The number of single-parent families has increased drastically in the past ten years with parenting being carried out in most cases by Mum. There has grown up, therefore, a generation whose direct experience of human fatherhood has either been completely lacking or very painful. Either way, images of fatherhood for many children have become negative and distorted.

In this situation it is hardly surprising that some Christians are discussing openly whether the fatherhood of God is an image that can be used. If a child has only a bad experience of fatherhood it is likely, they fear, that he or she will come (however unconsciously) to reject any teaching about God which majors upon the father image.

CONCLUSION
What can we say to this?

The first thing to emphasize is that despite negative experiences of human fatherhood, *healthy and positive images are still sufficiently common in society to make it possible for children without fathers, or with bad fathers, to grasp what good fatherhood is.* Even in areas where single-parent families are strong in number, most children have some direct experience of two-parent families. It is here we are helped by the emphasis in television programmes upon the normality of the typical two-parent, two-child family. Ministry to children in single-parent situations, then, needs to be sensitive (not least to Mum who may feel her singleness keenly) but it does not automatically rule out the use of father images for God.

The second point to remember is that *an understanding of God in motherly as well as fatherly terms will enable those involved in ministry to children and families to emphasize the motherly aspects where appropriate* without having to fall back on Mariology or the notion of the church as spiritual mother. If this seems a bit far-fetched we have only to recall that worship of Mary has flourished where the femininity of God has been denied and that Mothering Sunday originated as a recognition of Mother Church.

Thirdly, we need to recognize that *when we affirm both the femininity and masculinity of God we affirm the importance of human femininity and motherhood as well.* This can be crucial in single parent families where the head of the house is a woman. The fact that God possesses motherly characteristics gives value and dignity to the feminine dimension in its own right and not just as an attachment to, or extension of, the masculine. No longer can the positive qualities of parenthood be confined theologically to the father, for God himself is both heavenly Father and Mother.

Fourthly, we must acknowledge that despite all that has been said so far, *we are not free to sit loose to the image of God as Father.* The fact that the feminine dimension of God has been overlooked does not mean that we can *substitute* a purely feminine image for a purely masculine one. Biblically, both belong together and to play one off against the other would be disastrous. In our ministry to children and families we need constantly to stress that a true representation of God must contain both feminine *and* masculine characteristics; and that the qualities of the Godhead which we as individuals are called to reflect are both masculine and feminine.

ISSUE 2: Why the incarnation matters

The Sunday school at St Rubik's in the Cube is just like any other suburban Sunday school. It is well attended, and staffed by teachers who are genuinely concerned for the spiritual welfare of their children. A look at some of the children and teachers will give us an idea of what makes it tick.

Darren is nine. He comes from a home where consumer goods are the order of the day. Both his mum and dad go out to work to provide an abundance of mod-cons, gadgets and a new car every year. Darren not only has his own computer but a word processor as well, just so he can type his name in different letterings! In Darren's home, material possessions are not just a way of life but are the *goal* of life. The boundaries of life are set by the acquisition of consumer goods.

Tracey, on the other hand, is exactly the opposite. Her father is out of work and the family has only her mother's part-time earnings to rely on. So it is not surprising that Tracey is more than a bit envious of Darren. But she finds it a comfort that Jesus did not have a rich home. And, as her teacher says, God is more concerned about our souls and spirits than the possessions we have. For Tracey it's just as well.

Daniel is ten and comes from a secure Christian home. His parents go to church, read the Bible regularly and pray every day. They run a housegroup on Wednesday evenings where everybody compliments them on their comfortable home. It is a household where material goods and evangelical Christianity go hand in hand. Daniel has never thought about any other way of life and has never heard his parents do so either.

Now for the Sunday school staff.

Michael is a teacher by trade. A sound evangelical, he was converted while working in central London where he attended a famous West End church. His aim in Sunday school is straightforward: to preach conversion. He wants his class to be right with God and to witness to their friends and families. No lesson is complete unless it contains an evangelistic challenge. The cross lies at the centre of all his teaching. To Michael, the incarnation is just another piece of theological jargon.

Lucy is a card-carrying charismatic. She is 'into' renewal. Although she can be a bit intense at times, she has a likeable personality and gets on well with the children in her class. She is concerned to keep in tune with the Spirit and wants the children to enter into the fullness of the Spirit without being distracted by the lures of materialism and TV.

David works for a firm of City stockbrokers. He was converted in his teens at a camp run by the Christian Union at his public school. At Oxford he became president of the University Christian Union (the fifth from his school to do so since 1945). Recently, however, David has undergone a conversion to ecology. His house is now a cross between Habitat and Traidcraft. He and his wife eat only wholefoods and are keen on making raffia products. In the church they are known as the Raffia Mafia. David is keen to share this new-found way of life with the children in his class.

We are fortunate in having a record of the last teachers' planning session. Part of it went something like this:

Michael: I'm concerned the kids are drifting away from the gospel. They're becoming too wrapped up with the world.

David: But surely we have a responsibility to teach them about living in God's world. They have to learn how to use it properly.

Michael: Sure, as long as they come to Christ first. It's their souls that count after all.

Lucy: I agree with both of you but what we need is more teaching about the Spirit. Once the children are in tune with the Spirit they'll know what to do.

David: That's all right in theory but look at the way our kids are stuffed full of materialism. Darren is a prime example: on a good night the appliances in his home alone put the national grid into profit.

Lucy: The answer to materialism is clear teaching about the Spirit. When they are filled with the Spirit the children won't bother with material things. After all, the world and the flesh are in Satan's grasp and we need to engage in spiritual warfare to break their hold.

Michael: All this distracts us from our main task. We must preach the gospel. The cross is the antidote to the world. I think we should make sure each child hears about Calvary at every opportunity.

Our peek at St Rubik's may seem something of a parody but it is not too wide of the mark. The backgrounds and attitudes of Darren, Tracey and Daniel are typical of children who attend Sunday school in the average suburban church. They will be found in other types of church Sunday school too, but since the church is strongest in suburbia it is there that we will find the most typical examples. Similarly, Michael, Lucy and David represent in a slightly comical way different strands of modern church life.

Both sets of characters betray considerable confusion. For the adults it is confusion about the task of the Sunday school teacher; about the content of the Christian message; about the meaning of the gospel; about the relationship between the world and the kingdom; about the nature of the Christian life. If their teachers are so confused, it is inevitable that the children will reflect these confusions. But they are less concerned with theology and more troubled by practical questions. Tracey is a good example of this with her worries about material possessions.

What kind of theology would help both teachers and children to dispel their confusion? Among other things, the teachers and children at St Rubik's need to discover the truth of the *incarnation*.

Its centrality to Christianity

To speak of Jesus as God incarnate is to speak of a mystery. Of all Christian doctrines the incarnation is the most difficult for the modern mind to comprehend. Yet a Christianity without it is inconceivable. As Kenneth Leech has written: 'Without the incarnation, the belief in the Word made Flesh, there can be no Christianity, no Christian theology, no Christian spirituality.'[5]

These are strong words. But the church has always insisted on the centrality of the incarnation for a right understanding of Christ. In the New Testament we find the confession that 'Jesus Christ has come in the flesh' to have been the key test whenever anyone claimed to be inspired by the Spirit:

'Dear friends, do not believe every spirit, but test the spirits to see whether they are from God, because many false prophets have gone out into the world. This is how you can recognise the Spirit of God: Every spirit that acknowledges that Jesus Christ has come in the flesh is from God, but every spirit that does not acknowledge Jesus is not from God' (1 John 4:1–3).

Throughout the first four centuries, controversy raged about the person of Jesus. The period is littered with heresies condemned as destructive of the faith – Arianism, Docetism, Apollinarianism, to mention but three. Names which sound strange to us proved to be battlegrounds for the truth about Jesus. The fact that such controversy raged should alert us to the importance of the incarnation: it was (and is) not a matter of indifference but is central to the life of the church.

The question was settled in 451 at the famous Council of Chalcedon. It was here that a formula was developed which stated that Christ was 'truly God and truly man'. He was not a man who was simply special, nor was he a spirit-god who only took the appearance of a human being. He was, in some mysterious way, God in the flesh.

Incarnation and evangelism

For Michael, Lucy, David and the rest of us, all this might seem irrelevant. But the doctrine of the incarnation gives shape to our ministry in three distinctive and positive ways. As we compare these with the problems encountered by our fictional Sunday school teachers and children we shall see how relevant the incarnation is to modern evangelism. The incarnation reveals the following.

A God who loves all he has made

One of the effects of concentrating only on sin is to downgrade the value and dignity of God's creation. This includes human beings. The incarnation reminds us that the created order is of highest value to God. Why else would he have taken human form and participated in the life of his creatures? Both Michael and

Lucy run the risk of falling into the trap dug by the Gnostics, an early sect who regarded the material world as irrelevant to salvation. In fact, they did not merely regard the body and all things material as of no consequence, but condemned them as evil. Likewise, another group, the Arians, argued that God was so remote and transcendent that he could not possibly become a man. To do so would be to pollute himself with material existence which, by definition, God could not do.

From this it followed that Christ could not be fully God *and* fully man. He must have been either a man with an extraordinary spiritual dimension, a man endowed in an extra special way by the Spirit, or he must not have been a man at all but a spiritual being who took the form or appearance of a man – a kind of ghost who looked human. But whichever of these views was taken, it was clear that Jesus could not be understood as God in the flesh.

Michael and Lucy are not so extreme in their views but their attitudes make it plain that they both regard Christianity as something essentially inward – life lived in the Spirit. Michael is concerned with salvation as a matter of being right with God in our hearts and Lucy with the fullness of the Spirit. The created world is secondary, a necessary environment for us to live out our lives but one which pales into insignificance alongside the realm of the Spirit.

Francis Schaeffer has described this as the 'new super-spirituality'. He traces it to the ancient Greek philosophy of Platonism which regarded all material aspects of life as intrinsically inferior or even wicked. As a result, only the so-called 'spiritual' realm could be accepted as the sphere of God's activity:

'Because Platonism frowned on the body, the body was suspect, only the soul was good. Thus there was a tendency to act as if the only thing that matters is to see that a man's soul is saved so that it can go to heaven.'

Schaeffer accurately identified the result of this:

'The person disappears. Only the soul is valuable, and its value is in heaven and has very little to do with anything in the present life – the body, the intellect and the culture.'[6]

Michael and Lucy, who in their differing ways are so much like many Christians today, represent this 'new super-spirituality'. For them, the task of the Christian worker is to bring children to an inward spiritual salvation. Other things do not matter: God only cares about the spiritual side of life. The gospel and the Christian life are to do with inward conversion and trust in Jesus. The goal of the believer is to know God and to enjoy the life of the Spirit.

The incarnation knocks all this on the head. For Jesus did not come as a spirit disguised as a man, but as God himself in the flesh. This proves the commitment of God to the material order. So we must not see the incarnation simply as the necessary prelude to the cross, as if Jesus had to come as a man because we are sinners trapped in human bodies. His taking flesh was not a necessary evil – rather, the exact opposite. The incarnation was God's *affirmation* of the created world. He did not become flesh *in spite of* all that he had made but *because he loved it* and identified with it. The incarnation was God's restatement of his delight in creation: 'And God saw that it was good.'

A God who redeems all creation

Once we accept that God's love embraces the whole of the created order and not just that part we arbitrarily call 'spiritual', we are led to some far-reaching conclusions. The first and foremost of these is that we must reject the separation of life into two tiers – a higher, spiritual one which God cares about and redeems, and a lower, earthly tier, which is irrelevant or controlled by Satan and therefore unredeemed.

This two-tier thinking is destroyed by the incarnation. If God had intended only to redeem our spirits or souls, then the Docetists were right: Jesus was not God in the flesh and did not die in the flesh. He was a spirit who merely took the *appearance* of a man. But, as John both in his Gospel and his epistle reminds us, the confession that Jesus was God come in the flesh is the crucial test of whether our statements about him are true. Had God been concerned only with some kind of purely 'spiritual' redemption, then the incarnation was not only unnecessary, it was largely meaningless. It is only by understanding the significance of Jesus as God *in the flesh* that we fully perceive God's affirmation of material life. The redemption achieved on the cross covers not just our souls but the whole of creation. God becomes part of his world so that he might redeem it in its entirety.

In evangelism this means that we shall be careful not to underplay the fact that Jesus was both truly God and truly man. We shall neither present him as a supercharged miracle worker nor as an ethereal heavenly figure who happens to look human. We shall instead strive to bring home to children (and adults for that matter) that Jesus was God in the flesh, as we are in the flesh, and that this above all else demonstrates his love for us in every aspect of our lives. We shall cease to imply a false division between the spiritual and material. For both are embraced within the incarnation and both are the objects of God's love.

A God who is involved with the world

If we take the Bible seriously, we must reject any suggestion that God is too remote to have anything to do with the world. The writer to the Hebrews makes it clear that the very continuance of the world from day to day depends upon Christ's ongoing word of power:

'. . . in these last days [God] has spoken to us by his Son, whom he appointed heir of all things, and through whom he made the universe. The Son is the radiance of God's glory and the exact representation of his being, *sustaining all things by his powerful word*' (Heb 1:2–3).

The incarnation carries this insight one stage further. It says that by taking flesh, God committed himself to daily *human* life. By entering into the everyday experiences of ordinary people, he gave them abiding value, and a significance beyond measure.

But more than that, he made it clear that his love for the world and for its people was to be the model for his disciples. If they were to be his followers they would have to love as he loved. There was to be no room for faith or 'spiritual' experiences which were self-centred. The Holy Spirit would come not in order to bring gifts to 'enjoy', as if they were simply another pleasure, but to bring gifts of service that would build up others and demonstrate the presence of God.

In the same way, Jesus' miracles of feeding and healing take on incarnational significance. They were not merely demonstrations of power, or signs that the kingdom of God had arrived. They were evidence that the material order was to be loved and taken seriously. People were to be healed and fed because they were intrinsically valuable. God cared for their bodies because they were not simply embodied spirits but whole persons, and as whole persons reflected the image of God. As Gregory Palamas has commented, 'The word Man is not applied to either soul or body separately but to both together, since together they have been created in the image of God.'[7]

The most obvious evangelistic implication is that if God loved the world and identified with it by taking flesh then we must love it too, and not just for the sake of redeeming souls. Here is Kenneth Leech again:

'A major consequence of taking incarnational faith seriously is that the spiritual person, far from despising or fearing or withdrawing from the world, needs to be inflamed by a passionate and intense love for the world, seeing in the material things of the world that handiwork of God, and in the people of the world the face of Christ.'[8]

Michael and Lucy, then, veer towards a faith and a gospel which does not take the incarnation seriously. Like many Christians they are doing so without realizing it and from the best of motives. But in the task of living the truth, motives are not enough: the *preaching* of the gospel must conform to the *truth* of the gospel, and that means being true to the fullness of the incarnation.

Applying the insights

Finally, let's consider what it would mean if we were to apply incarnational insights to our Sunday school teaching programme. (This might well also apply to an adult-centred programme.)

The first difference would be that we would stop talking about the world as if it were outside the sphere of God's loving concern. We would learn to speak of it positively, as valuable to God in its own material right and not just the place where millions of unsaved souls happen to reside.

Secondly, we would enthuse our children with a love for the created order as the handiwork of God. The world, its life, and human life are to be rejoiced in because they belong to God and are the result of his work. If God saw that his creation was good, so can we.

Thirdly, we would encourage our children to receive gladly the good things that God has given them but not to become wrapped up with them. Part of Tracey's problem was that the attitude of her Sunday school teacher forced her to choose *between* material things and the life of the Spirit. The incarnation teaches us that the material and the spiritual do not have to be set against each other.

Fourthly, we would enable our children to see that gifts from God, both material and spiritual, have to be used wisely and not selfishly. This would rule out the acquisition of possessions simply for their own sake or to keep up with the Joneses. It would put possessions firmly in their place – to be used for the service of others.

Fifthly and lastly, we would share with our children our own burning concern for God's world and its people; a concern that results from our understanding of the incarnation. We would long for their attitude and ours to be that of Isaac the Syrian, who lived in the seventh century:

'What is a charitable heart? It is a heart which is burning with love for the whole creation, for men, for the birds, for the beasts, for the demons – for all creatures. He who has such a heart cannot see or call to mind a creature without his eyes being filled with tears by reason of the immense compassion which seizes his heart; a heart which is softened and can no longer bear to see or learn from others of any suffering, even the smallest pain, being inflicted upon a creature. That is why such a man never ceases to pray also for the animals, for the enemies of truth and for those who do him evil. . .'[9]

CONCLUSION

Evangelism powered by this kind of incarnational faith would bring revolution in its wake! Individual lives would be transformed, communities healed, and God's world treated with reverence by Christians whose lives had been touched by the love with which *God* loves his creation. We would learn to love with an incarnational love that refuses to allow the church to become a spiritual ghetto or the gospel to become a mere mechanism for saving souls. In short, Christ's followers would become Christlike: Christ in the flesh.

The incarnation is crucial, then, not simply as a doctrine to be believed but as a truth to be lived. It undergirds our evangelism (both to children and adults) by giving *content* to our understanding of who Jesus was and God's relationship to the world, and by providing a *model* for the kind of persons we must be if we are to present the gospel credibly and effectively. When we, as Christians, actively incarnate the love of God as Christ incarnated the love of his Father, then those who see Christ in us will have been confronted with the authentic heart of the gospel.

ISSUE 3: Children and the Spirit

'Do not quench the Spirit,' said Paul to the Thessalonian Christians twenty years after Christ's death (1 Thess 5:19; RSV). Two thousand years later, there are many millions of people touched by the renewal movement for whom this text has become a watchword. When Anglican bishops are publicly seen to dance in the Spirit, we know something has happened! What started out in modern times as a trickle at the edges of the church's life has turned into a mighty river sweeping through its core.

But the debate has moved on to a new stage. The theology as well as the fact of spiritual gifts (charismata) has been widely accepted. The practices of speaking in tongues, interpretation, prophecy and other gifts mentioned by Paul are no longer dismissed as the unbalanced enthusiasm of a few cranks and weirdos. Many churches have incorporated them into their life and worship.

In the mainstream denominations this has been confined largely to adults. Now a further question is being asked: are spiritual gifts for children too? Should we encourage youngsters to seek and receive them? More specifically, should evangelism include an exhortation to seek charismata as well as salvation?

The case for encouraging children to receive the Spirit's gifts might run something like this:

1. The gifts are Spirit-given blessings to the people of God. Children count as God's people no less than adults. The gifts are therefore intended for both children and adults.

2. Spiritual gifts are part of the experience of belonging to Christ and being 'in him'. Jesus said that children belonged to him and rebuked those who tried to stop children from reaching him. This surely means that they are inheritors of his blessings. These include spiritual gifts.

3. All Christians receive the Holy Spirit when they receive Christ. When children receive Christ, they likewise receive the Spirit, which means receiving his gifts too.

4. If children are capable of receiving the gift of salvation, they are capable also of receiving gifts of the Spirit.

There is a certain coherence about these arguments: they seem to make a great deal of sense. But is that really the case? How do we go about evaluating them? The issue is so controversial that we cannot avoid having to engage in some tough theological reasoning.

We shall look principally at New Testament discussion of spiritual gifts to see if we can find any clues which will help us in our quest. The kind of questions we shall be concerned with include: what is the nature of spiritual gifts? What is their purpose? Does their character mean that they are intended only for adults or could we envisage the New Testament sanctioning their use by children? Are there any explicit principles which would either forbid or encourage children to exercise them?

These are large questions. But they must be set alongside insights afforded by the study of child development. If we accept that every person goes through stages of faith which are related to physical, social and psychological development, how do these fit with either the experience of charismata or a theology of gifts? The New Testament must be our basic resource for answering theological questions and must be the final authority in matters of faith, but we must also ask how theology and experience relate to what we know about human growth and development.

These are questions we shall be examining in some detail in the course of this chapter. Our method will be twofold: the majority of the discussion will focus upon the theological issues involved; the remainder will look at the questions from the standpoint of child development. At the end we shall summarize our conclusions from both angles.

Insights from the New Testament

The New Testament as a whole is not very much concerned about spiritual gifts. Most of its teaching on the subject can be found in the writings of Paul, notably chapters twelve to fourteen of his first letter to the Corinthians. It is here that we find a detailed theology which furnishes some guidelines for the use of gifts in the church.

It is interesting to reflect how much we would know about

charismata if Corinth had not been a problem congregation. For Paul's discussion of gifts does not take the form of abstract theological propositions but a series of points to deal with specific difficulties. What we have, then, is not so much a prospectus or a maker's manual about how to develop spiritual gifts, but a number of responses to a particularly complex situation. This should caution us against reading Paul's comments as a set of rules which can be simply lifted out of the context for which they were written and plonked down upon a late twentieth-century church in a very different situation. Nevertheless, once we have got this fact into our heads, it becomes possible to trace continuities between Corinth and ourselves so that we can at least find some clues to aid us in our search. The first task must be for us to reconstruct, as far as possible, the context of Paul's writing.

What kind of church existed at Corinth?

Corinth was a great sea port. It controlled the land route from north to south and the sea route from east to west. It was a bustling city full of corruption. Its reputation for immorality went back a century and had been so great that it spawned a new word for excess and sexual licence: to corinthianize.

Christians converted from paganism had to resist not only the city's corruption but the effects of pagan worship. Sacrifices to idols were commonplace and the town was dominated by the temple of Aphrodite, the goddess of love, with her thousands of temple prostitutes.

It is little wonder, then, that the church at Corinth was beset with problems. In the course of his letter, we find Paul dealing with: divisions, factions and party jealousies (1:11–13); some members taking others to court (6:1–8); a notorious case of incest (5:1–5); sex outside marriage, even between Christians and prostitutes (6:15–20); disputes over food offered to idols (8:1–13); gluttony at the Lord's Supper at which people guzzled the bread and wine like animals (11:17–22); chaos in worship (14:33); lack of love (13); denial of Christ's resurrection (15:12); and questioning of Paul's apostleship (4:1–3,15; 9:1–2). In short, the Corinthian church was an unholy, unspiritual mess.

This was the context in which spiritual gifts were operating.

It is worth noting that Paul does not deny the validity of such gifts on the grounds of the church's unspirituality. He does not say that such people could never exercise gifts. After all, Paul had laid the foundation of the Corinthian church (3:10) and knew that despite the problems there remained a genuineness of faith. As C K Barrett comments: 'He neither denies the right of such phenomena to exist within the church nor affirms that in themselves they are proof of the presence and activity of the Spirit of God.'[10]

But this does not mean that Paul uncritically accepted every claim to a spiritual gift simply because someone felt the Spirit come upon them. He calls instead for a mature discernment of the true from the false. The key to this, he reminds his readers, is the relationship between the believer and Christ.

'Now about spiritual gifts, brothers, I do not want you to be ignorant . . . no-one can say, "Jesus is Lord," except by the Holy Spirit' (1 Cor 12:1,3).

What Paul is *not* saying is that the mere formula 'Jesus is Lord' shows a person's true obedience to Christ – anybody can parrot the words. Rather, the life of the Christian who claims to possess a gift reflects his submission to the lordship of Jesus in all its spiritual and ethical dimensions. Only when accompanied by a life of genuine Christ-likeness, should a gift be counted as authentically inspired by God's Spirit. As Barrett comments:

'The true Christian watchword is *Jesus is Lord*. . . It is true not because it is the right or orthodox formula but because it expresses the proper relationship with Jesus: the speaker accepts his authority and proclaims himself the servant of him whom he confesses as Lord.'[11]

The Corinthians have to recognize, therefore, that some of their gifts may be counterfeit and that merely claiming to speak under the inspiration of the Spirit is not enough. The reason for Paul's caution is that ecstatic gifts, especially tongues, were part and parcel of pagan worship. Some of the Christians in Corinth who had been converted from paganism may well have exercised pagan spiritual gifts in their former religion. Paul is concerned, therefore, to urge the Corinthians not to accept claims to inspiration uncritically, but to assess whatever is said or done by a number of simple tests. This is what lies behind his statement: 'You know when you were heathen you were led astray to dumb idols, however you may have been moved' (12:2; RSV). It was possible for a person to exercise what appeared to be a spiritual gift and yet be acting not according to the Spirit of God but out of a hangover from pagan days or at the promptings of the Deceiver.

The tests of authenticity

For Paul, then, feelings were not the decisive evidence of authenticity. The person who claimed to possess a gift of the Spirit must be willing to submit to a fourfold test:

1. *The life of the believer must be consistent* with his claim to be led by God. Paul was not looking for perfection but for evidence of the fruits as well as the gifts of the Spirit. There must be a match between the attitudes and life of the believer on one hand and his alleged gift on the other. The key to this was love. The Christian who claimed a gift such as tongues or prophecy, for example, but whose life demonstrated a lack of love either did not possess the genuine article or needed further teaching. Either way, he would be insensitive and brash like a gong or a clanging cymbal (13:1) – however eloquent he might be.

We can see this point worked out in detail in Paul's letters to the Ephesians and the Galatians. In both places (Eph 4 and 5; Gal 5), he stresses that to live in the Spirit doesn't just mean experiencing the gifts of the Spirit but also entails the fruit of the Spirit. The characteristics of a fruit-filled life are love, joy, peace, patience, kindness, goodness, faithfulness, gentleness, self-control (Gal 5:22–23), combined with lowliness, meekness, forbearing one another, and eagerness to maintain the unity of the Spirit in the bond of peace (Eph 4:1–3).

These are all the fruits of maturity. They are not optional extras but the evidence of authentic Christian experience. Paul is well aware that they are not fruits which can grow overnight but nevertheless he is insistent that those who claim the Spirit must show the fruits as well as the gifts if their claim is to be taken seriously.

2. *The content of a gift must conform to Christian truth.* Hence, 'no-one who is speaking by the Spirit of God says, "Jesus be cursed" ' (12:3). Significantly, elsewhere in the New Testament we find similar tests (1 John 4:1–3).

3. *A gift must edify or build up the church.* We shall deal with this in more detail later.

4. *A gift must be evaluated by others in the church* (14:29). There are three possible meanings of this verse:

(a) a gift should be assessed by those who possess the same gift (prophets should test prophecy, healers healings etc);

(b) a gift should be tested by the general leadership of the church;

(c) a gift should be tested by the congregation as a whole.

It is not clear from the text which of these Paul had in mind, but the underlying point remains: gifts should be tested by mature, responsible members of the church and not just accepted on the say-so of the claimant. This is a crucial point of pastoral practice.

The situation at Corinth, then, was complex and peculiar. Side by side with immorality, false teaching and unspirituality we find spiritual gifts. This leads us to ask a second question.

What kind of people should exercise gifts?

In Paul's view, the only people whose claims to possess spiritual gifts should be taken seriously are those whose lives are ethically and spiritually mature. It is here that we find an illuminating reference by the apostle to the place of children. In 14:20, Paul likens the spiritual immaturity of the Corinthians to the natural immaturity of children:

'Brothers, stop thinking like children [*paidia*]. In regard to evil be infants, but in your thinking be adults.'

The significance of this verse is that it appears in the middle of Paul's discussion of the conditions required for the legitimate exercise of charismata. By comparing the Corinthians with children, he is saying that by nature children are immature. But the Corinthians are not to be like children in their practice of spiritual gifts – they are to show adult maturity. This alone is fitting.

The contrast Paul makes between children and maturity suggests that children are too immature, in general, to exercise gifts of the Spirit. Of course, there may be exceptions, but the maturity required for the proper use of charismata is an essentially adult quality. If this is not an implication of 14:20, it is difficult to see what is.

What Paul means by immaturity can be seen from his earlier comments in chapter 3. He had used the image of childhood as a warning to his readers:

'Brothers, I could not address you as spiritual but as worldly – mere infants in Christ. I gave you milk not solid food, for you were not yet ready for it. Indeed, you are still not ready. You are still worldly. For since there is jealousy and quarrelling among you, are you not worldly? Are you not acting like mere men?' (1 Cor 3:1–3.)

Immaturity, then, is the failure to live ethically, to recognize that the lordship of Christ requires a new way of living. Maturity, on the other hand, is reflected in a genuinely Christ-like humility and love. This, in turn, requires an adult understanding of the death and resurrection of Christ, the significance of the Spirit and the meaning of the scriptures (4:6).

All this presupposes adult capabilities. This is not to say that children cannot trust in Christ or know the work of his Spirit in their lives. But this will be at a level appropriate to the natural immaturity of the child years.

The possession and use of spiritual gifts, argues Paul, must be accompanied by a mature demonstration of fruits of the Spirit. Taken together, they presuppose a maturity which lies beyond the capabilities of childhood.

What are the gifts for?

In his dialogue with the Corinthians, Paul tackles two common but mistaken notions of the purpose of charismata. We need to take note of what he says because they are used today to justify the seeking of spiritual gifts both for children and adults.

Mistake number one: Charismata are given to prove the presence of God to unbelievers.

This view is widespread especially in relation to healing. 'Signs and wonders' ministry in particular assumes that spectacular manifestations of supernatural power will convince the unbeliever of the truth of the gospel and drive him to faith. Urging us to see this as normative for evangelism today, John Wimber writes that, 'through these supernatural encounters people experience the presence and power of God . . . resistance to the gospel is supernaturally overcome and receptivity to Christ's claims is usually very high.'[12]

This is not the place to discuss the theology of power evangelism in detail but if it is true that the primary purpose of charismata is evangelistic then we can see how their use with children might be defended. However, while we must accept that God in his grace does speak to unbelievers through the use of spiritual gifts, we must also recognize that a careful reading of 1 Corinthians 12 and 14 should make us cautious before we promote them as normal evangelistic tools. Let's spell this out.

Nowhere in either chapter does Paul suggest that the primary purpose of gifts is evangelism. The two gifts he does discuss because of their effect on unbelievers are tongues and prophecy. But even here, he says their results will be contradictory. If outsiders hear tongues in worship, they will be confirmed in their unbelief: 'will they not say that you are out of your mind?' (14:23.) If they hear prophecy, they will be convicted and turn to God: 'he will fall down and worship God, exclaiming "God is really among you!" ' (14:25.)

This is the closest Paul comes to an evangelistic interpretation of spiritual gifts. But even so, it is mighty thin ice to skate on. It will not bear the weight put upon it by the signs and wonders school for a number of reasons.

Firstly, if the apostle believed charismata were given primarily for power evangelism, why did he not lay down a much fuller exposition of this with some clear guidelines for their use in evangelistic contexts? He had gone out of his way to set out rules for the ordering of church life and the proper use of gifts in worship. Why not for evangelism? It is simply not credible given the state of the Corinthian fellowship with all its confusion, unspirituality and immaturity that Paul would have omitted to give teaching on this vital aspect, had the gifts been intended primarily for evangelism.

Secondly, although Paul notes that prophecy can convince unbelievers of God's presence, he does not argue for it as a normative evangelistic weapon. His aim is something quite different: it is to show the Corinthians who were hooked on tongues and prophecy that, of the two, prophecy was more desirable because it was more intelligible. Significantly, he states in 14:19 (RSV) that he 'would rather speak five words with my mind in order to instruct others, than ten thousand words in a tongue.' When Paul says that prophecy convinces outsiders, therefore, he is not advocating its use as a means of witness: he is simply trying to steer the Corinthians away from their obsession with tongues. 'If you must place such heavy reliance on charismata,' he is saying, 'then promote prophecy rather than tongues because at least it can be understood.' This is a far cry from advocating it as part of a programme of power evangelism.

Thirdly, the overwhelming burden of Paul's teaching in Corinthians is concerned not with soul-winning but with building up the church. This points to a second false idea about spiritual gifts.

Mistake number two: Gifts are primarily for personal enjoyment; they carry the believer into a new stage of spiritual life where his walk with God and spirituality are deepened and enriched.

The essential error in this view is that it mistakes the by-product of a gift (personal enjoyment by the possessor) for the fundamental purpose (edification of the whole body of Christ). Paul is adamant that gifts are given for the good of the church rather than the benefit of the possessor: 'to each one the manifestation of the Spirit is given *for the common good*' (12:7). 'Since you are eager to have spiritual gifts, try to excel in gifts that *build up the church*' (14:12).

Paul underlines his point by explaining the purpose of the gift of tongues. These are important, he contends, but they must always be used so that others may be built up. They are not simply for private consumption. It is no good babbling away in unintelligible noises just for your own sake. Such an activity may make you feel good but it runs counter to the basic reason for which gifts were given: the edification of others. At the very least, the tongue speaker in worship should pray for an interpretation (14:13) but if there is no recognized interpreter in the congregation the gift should not be used (14:28). Even better (says Paul) let tongues give way to prophecy which can be understood by all.

These may seem harsh words but in the muddled and unbalanced context of Corinth they were necessary. Paul's purpose is to see that the gifts of the Spirit are used for the benefit of all and not just a few.

What does he mean when he speaks of upbuilding or edification? Paul has in mind two kinds of Christians: (a) those who claim gifts in order to indulge and draw attention to themselves ('Look how great I am, I speak in tongues'); and (b) those whose gifts point the onlooker away from the user to God or to the needs of others. Gifts which edify are those which achieve the latter purpose: they encourage, strengthen and challenge. They are not part of an ego-trip.

How is this to be achieved? Paul gives his answer by contrasting tongues with prophecy. The Corinthians had elevated tongues to the supreme place among charismata. Unless you spoke in tongues you could not be regarded as spiritual. Paul turns this view on its head, first by putting tongues at the end, not the beginning, of his list of gifts in chapter 12; and second, by comparing them to prophecy.

Prophecy is portrayed as an example of the true purpose of gifts because 'everyone who prophesies speaks to men for their strengthening, encouragement and comfort. He who speaks in a tongue edifies himself but he who prophesies edifies the church' (14:3–4). The superiority of prophecy lies, therefore, in its capacity to benefit the whole church and not just the one who utters it. Moreover, it serves as the model for other gifts: they should all aim at mutual upbuilding. 'Since you are eager to have spiritual gifts, try to excel in gifts that build up the church' (14:12). These words addressed to the early Christians also address us today.

What about children?

How does all this relate to children? The first point to make is that in the whole of Paul's teaching on spiritual gifts it is striking that he nowhere raises the question of how children should seek or exercise them. He assumes that they are to be used only by adults. Children are conspicuous by their absence except to be held up as examples of immaturity which Christians are to avoid. As with the question of spiritual gifts and evangelism, we have to recognize that if they had been intended for use by children it is astonishing that Paul has nothing to say about it. Rules are apparently necessary for the use of gifts by adults but not by children despite all that he says about their natural immaturity!

Secondly, we have to remember what gifts are and are not for. We have already seen that their purpose is neither to impress non-Christians nor to boost the possessor. So it is no good arguing for children to seek them on the grounds that gifts will convert them to Christ or deepen their walk with God. For reasons which will become clear when we consider insights from child development, pushing children to receive charismata is more likely to produce long-term spiritual casualties than long-term spiritual fruit. If we have been entrusted with the spiritual and psychological well-being of young people, we must not play fast and loose with their hearts and minds simply to satisfy our own theological or spiritual egos.

Thirdly, it is difficult to see how the goal which Paul has in mind for spiritual gifts – the edification of the church – can readily be fulfilled through children in the way in which Paul intends. When he speaks of edification, he associates it with the activities of strengthening, encouragement and comfort, all of which require adult capacities of understanding, ministry and teaching. For at the centre of edification lies the ministry of God's word, spoken, as Paul stresses, *with the mind*. This is the point, as we have seen, of his comparison of tongues with prophecy. One edifies more readily because it is intelligent and intelligible. The other less so.

Once we grasp the logic of Paul's argument, we have a major problem with the view that children should be encouraged to seek gifts of the Spirit. The maturity of mind and spirit which a proper exercise of the gifts presupposes is only rarely to be found in children. The person who is able to edify others is the person who is able to interpret the mind of God to his hearers. This requires a structure of mind and spirit which is essentially adult.

The alternative is to hold a 'hosepipe' view of inspiration. According to this, the possessor of a gift is entirely passive in the operation of the gift. God simply channels his power through him rather like a gardener channels water from the tap to the garden via the home. In neither case does the channel have anything to do with what goes through it. It is no more than a passive instrument.

This is the idea many Christians hold of charismata: the believer is a conduit for the power of God rather than a creative partner with whom God has chosen to work. If this were true, it could be argued that children can just as easily be channels for divine inspiration as adults. But this proves too much: if inspiration is simply a matter of being a spiritual hosepipe why should we limit the use of gifts to children? Why not animals, on the precedent of Balaam's ass?

This is not the nature of inspiration. Thinking that it was, led the Corinthians to elevate tongues above everything else. Paul's emphasis on the use of the mind and his preference for prophecy were designed to make clear that the exercise of spiritual gifts was not a matter of empty passivity. The gifts are controllable by their possessors and subject to their wills. That is why Paul can tell his audience that if there is no interpreter present in worship, the tongue-speaker should keep quiet *no matter how moved he might feel* (14:28). Similarly, he affirms that 'the spirits of the prophets are subject to the control of prophets' (14:32).

Gifts in the context of worship

There remains one final point which is relevant to children. The only systematic New Testament teaching on spiritual gifts sets them in a particular context: the worship of God's people. The only structure which Paul recognizes for the regular use of charismata is the organized worship of the Body of Christ. In Paul's theology, it is the people of God gathered for worship who are the expression of Christ's Body. It is through the life of God's people in the fellowship of the local church that the Spirit ministers. This is why Paul gives rules for the conduct of worship and specifies God-given orders of ministry, in which those who possess spiritual gifts are included (12:28). The normal place for the exercise of gifts must be the church under the oversight of recognized spiritual leaders.

Now this is exactly what children's missions, Sunday schools and weekday clubs are not. They have neither the cross-section of age or experience that Paul presupposes in the church, nor do they have the maturity. Their purpose and leadership are entirely different from those of a church. If you are going to argue for child tongue-speakers, prophets and healers, then you will also have to argue for child apostles, teachers, pastors, administrators and so on. In Paul's mind they are inseparable. It is from those who possess spiritual gifts that leadership must arise for there is an intimate connection between the two.

The theological case for encouraging children to seek and exercise charismata, then, is full of problems: it cannot be found at all in the New Testament; its absence from the only systematic teaching we have on gifts is glaring; it conflicts with the nature and purpose of gifts; it overlooks the need for maturity which lies beyond children; it cannot be easily reconciled with a biblical understanding of the church. Given these considerable problems it is difficult to mount a convincing case for the practice of child-centred spiritual gifts.

Insights from child development
Whichever model of child development we take, it is clear that adult maturity does not begin to emerge until late adolescence. It would seem, then, that Paul grasped intuitively what we can now show scientifically: that to encourage children to seek and exercise spiritual gifts is inappropriate to the general sequence of growth and development. Of course, there may be exceptions as God chooses to fill a child with the Spirit for a particular purpose. But this is not the same thing as supposing that it is God's *general* will for all children. There are four specific areas which point to the inappropriateness of a child's exercise of spiritual gifts.

1. Magic

It is not a great step from seeing spectacular supernatural gifts as the hand of God to thinking of them as magic. This can be particularly true of healings where *the healer* seems to possess untold powers which he can summon up at will by the recitation of a formula which sounds suspiciously like a spell. Such a confusion (which is not unknown among adults) is characteristic, as we have seen, of the junior years. Children are prone to interpret any spiritual gift as magical simply because the intellectual, emotional and spiritual framework that enables a mature understanding to take place is not yet present. The child inevitably thinks in magical categories. An evangelist or Christian worker who exhorts a child to receive and practise a spiritual gift, therefore, must be aware that he is playing with fire. Children are led into all kinds of theological, spiritual and psychological problem areas.

2. Emotional disturbance

This is arguably the most dangerous of the problem areas mentioned above. Childhood and adolescence are periods of rapid emotional growth. But they are also the periods of greatest turmoil and confusion as the child struggles to find meaning, identity and security. It is easy to exploit this vulnerability, wittingly or unwittingly, by pushing spiritual gifts. Their very nature – dramatic, powerful, supernatural – is immensely appealing. But without an accompanying maturity, they can be enormously disruptive of stable emotional development. At the very worst, particularly in mass meetings, they can be vehicles for manipulation. Exhortations therefore to be 'slain in the Spirit' and other so-called spiritual acts are irresponsible and potentially damaging. In any other context they might well be regarded as scandalous. Those who defiantly promote such activities may have much to answer for in later years of development.

A related point is that of authority and responsibility. In a church setting, the minister has a recognized authority. He or she is chosen for (among other things) his wisdom and maturity. He holds authority because he is the recognized leader and is appointed to carry ultimate responsibility for actions which take place within the church. Moreover, if he is a good minister, he will know his congregation (including the children) and will be in a position to evaluate their needs.

In a mission or similar setting, however, the situation is different. Leaders will know very little about the children they meet and will almost certainly not have any ongoing responsibility for them. This can give rise to a great temptation to 'play God' and encourage attitudes and reactions among children which would be unacceptable in a regular church context. The general rule should be: when on mission, encourage only those reactions and consequences for which both you and the host church would be prepared to take responsibility and be accountable in an ongoing church situation. If neither you nor they would do it as part of regular ministry, don't do it!

3. Intellectual understanding

Much contemporary research suggests that children may not be capable of the necessary acts of understanding and control of spiritual gifts except in rare cases. 'Speaking with the mind' involves knowing how to relate a gift to the truth about Christ; handling scripture in a mature way; and the capacity to speak words that strengthen, encourage and comfort the hearer. We must say, once more, that from a developmental point of view, these abilities are not present until the onset of adulthood. This is not the same as saying that the gifts are only for intellectuals (God forbid!) but there must be a basic level of adult understanding and maturity.

4. Adult power

To a child, an adult is like a god: his word is authoritative and his actions all-powerful. The adult who promotes spiritual gifts, therefore, must realize what he is doing: he, the knowledgeable, unchallengeable authority-figure is saying, either implicitly or explicitly, that the child's Christian experience will not be complete until he has sought these things. But the adult is also saying something else: that *he*, the leader, wants the child to seek a spiritual gift. The child will understand from this that if he is to please the adult, he will do what he says.

It is but a short step to manufacture the required phenomenon. It is a well-known fact (I have experienced it myself) that adolescents can produce tongues or some other kind of inspired utterance in order to please a youth leader or pastor. We should not fool ourselves and should consequently refrain from putting children and adolescents under such pressure.

There is another factor, however. Junior and adolescent youngsters are great peer group affiliators (Westerhoff) and conformists (Fowler). If one member of a group appears to receive a gift, others will soon follow. This is inevitable. But it can lead to delusions of revival as leaders begin to think that a massive spiritual revolution is under way. More often than not, it is simply another example of the affiliative stage and should be treated in a low-key manner.

CONCLUSION

I have argued in favour of spiritual gifts but not for their promotion among children. In my view, the biblical, theological and developmental evidence suggests that they are appropriate only for adults. In saying this, I am aware that there will be those who have witnessed the exercise of charismatic-style phenomena by children and who will therefore reject my arguments. To them I can only say: (a) I do not rule out the exceptional or occasional use of spiritual gifts by children but I do question whether they should ever be regarded as normative; (b) the balance of theological evidence weighs against the association of gifts with children; and (c) even if the theological questions could be adequately dealt with, the developmental questions still remain. In short, the difficulties both theological and developmental cannot be wished away simply by appealing to spectacular experiences which may have other theological and psychological explanations.

NOTES TO CHAPTER 9

1. J Jeremias, *The Prayers of Jesus*, London: SCM 1967, p 29.
2. Jeremias, as above, p 63.
3. Since writing this chapter I have been persuaded by Mary Hayter's argument that feminine language about God must not be pressed too hard, lest more be read into the biblical references than can be

189

justified. I recommend her book, *The New Eve in Christ* (London: SPCK 1987), especially chapters One and Two, as a thoroughly biblical examination of the theological issues discussed in this chapter.

4. P Craigie, *The Book of Deuteronomy*, London: Hodder & Stoughton 1976, p 333.
5. Kenneth Leech, *True God*, London: Sheldon Press 1985, p 236.
6. Francis A Schaeffer, *The New Super-Spirituality*, London: Hodder & Stoughton 1973, pp 20–21.
7. Quoted in Leech, as above, p 242.
8. Leech, as above, p 245.
9. Quoted in Leech, as above, p 246.
10. C K Barrett, *The First Epistle to the Corinthians*, London: A & C Black, 1973, p 279.
11. Barrett, as above, p 281.
12. John Wimber, *Power Evangelism*, London: Hodder & Stoughton, 1985, p 46.

Afterword

We have reached the end of this book but not of our learning. As our ministry to children moves on, we shall, if we are attentive to the Spirit of God, be always ready to discern new insights and revise old ones. But as we close this study, I should like to set out three convictions which have been central throughout and which have grown in strength as I have continued writing:

1. Children are infinitely precious to God

This is not just a piece of the sentimentality which characterizes modern attitudes to children. It is a hard theological fact: the Son of God gave himself for the sons and daughters of men so that they might become children of God. The incarnation of Jesus as both child and adult underlines the commitment and identification of the eternal God with all the phases of our human growth and development. Jesus was child as well as man.

2. We have a tremendous responsibility to fulfil

If God has acted in love towards children, then so must we. We must never regard them merely as miniature adults or souls to win. They are persons, each in his or her own right, and each made in God's image. This does not mean we have to be indulgent or naive: children too share in human flawedness and sin. But our responsibility is to love, cherish and care. As a result we shall be careful never to manipulate young minds or hearts, even from the best of intentions. As adults we shall be conscious both of their vulnerability and of our power. Our evangelism will reflect our awareness that we are no more than stewards of the gospel and shepherds of God's flock. We are not sheepdogs whose purpose is to round children up into the pen of our own making. God will not thank us for that.

3. God has entrusted us with the task of understanding

This will involve a willingness to grapple with both theology and child development. The easiest thing in the world would now be to put this book down and go back to ministry as if nothing had changed. Only when we struggle with trying to match with our experience the difficult questions thrown up by the study of child development, and then try to think about both theologically, will we find that God opens our hearts and minds to something new. If we are determined that we have nothing new to learn then God will simply let us be confirmed in our refusal. If, however, we are ready humbly and honestly to bring ourselves and our questions to him, he will give us answers in due course. That is the conviction and message of this book.